Work and Society:
An Introduction to Industrial Sociology

Work
and
Society

An Introduction to Industrial Sociology

Second Edition

Curt Tausky

University of Massachusetts at Amherst

 F. E. Peacock Publishers, Inc.
Itasca, Illinois 60143

To Coleman, Emily, and Philip

Copyright © 1996
F.E. Peacock Publishers, Inc.
All rights reserved
Library of Congress Catalog Card No. 95-72867
ISBN 0-87581-401-8
Printed in the U.S.A.
Printing   1 2 3 4 5 6 7 8 9 10
Year   00 99 98 97 96

Contents

Preface   ix

**1. Looking Back: Prehistoric, Ancient, and Medieval
     Societies**   **1**
     Introduction: Industrial Society and Industrial
          Sociology   1
     Hunting-Gathering Societies   2
     The Agricultural Revolution   4
     City-States and Empires: The Emergence of Elites   6
          Sumerian City-States   6
          State Proprietorship in Egypt   9
          The Roman Empire   12
     The Middle Ages   14
          The Manorial System   14
          The Guild System in Towns   17
          The Putting-Out System   20
     Summary   22

2. Looking Back: The Industrial Revolution   **23**
     Industrialization in England   24
          Industrial Developments   24
          Innovations in Transportation and Communication   27
          Social Effects of Industrialization   28
     Industrialization in the United States   34
          Industry, Commerce, and Agriculture   34
          Big Business   37
     Summary   42

3. **The Labor Force: Making a Living**   **44**
    Labor Force Participation   45
    Occupations   46
        Who Gets Which Jobs?   49
    Service-Producing and Goods-Producing Industries   51
    Other Sectors of the Labor Force   54
        Unemployment   54
        Underemployment and the Contingent Workforce   55
    Work Outcomes   59
        Income   61
        Prestige   74
        Job Satisfaction   75
    Summary   82

4. **Changing Work Outcomes**   **84**
    Occupational Mobility   84
        Intragenerational Mobility and Labor Turnover   84
        Intergenerational Mobility   86
    Unions and Collective Bargaining   89
        The Legal Framework   90
        The National Labor Relations Board   93
        The Growth and Decline of Unions   95
        Collective Bargaining   98
        Prospects for Labor Organizations   102
    Summary   104

5. **Overview: Looking Back and Ahead**   **105**
    Retrospect   105
        The Good Times, 1950–1975, and After   106
        From Dominant to One among Equals   108
        Industrial Structures   109
    Prospects   114
        The High-Performance Workplace   114
        Global Reach   120
        The Twenty-first Century   122

References   124

Index   135

Preface

Selecting materials for a concise book such as *Work and Society* demands many choices. My guide was the question, Which information, theories, and issues are important for understanding work and workplaces in this period of global competition? The first two chapters, which provide some historical background for what follows, are quite similar to those in the first edition of this book. Chapters 3 through 5, however, are heavily revised in this second edition. They have been largely or completely rewritten, and all the data have been updated.

Chapter 1 discusses early societies, and the manorial, guild, and putting-out systems of production that preceded the factory. Chapter 2 describes the Industrial Revolution in England and the United States. Chapter 3 examines key work outcomes—income, prestige, and job satisfaction—as well as occupational distributions, poverty, and so on. Whenever feasible, current data are shown in the context of several decades. Chapter 4 turns to occupational mobility, labor law, and labor unions. Chapter 5 explains how America's present economic circumstances emerged from Cold War rebuilding and trade strategies. It discusses systems of commercial enterprise that differ from the American pattern and considers occupations and incomes in the years ahead. When useful, the economic setting, such as the actions of the Federal Reserve Board, is introduced.

I have used drafts of these chapters in my undergraduate and graduate courses on industrial sociology, and introductory sociology. This rather wide range of readers had no difficulty in understanding the materials.

My sincere thanks to colleagues Randall Stokes, Chris Hurn, and Al Chevan for sharing with me their coffee and reflections on the economy; my publisher, Ted Peacock, for gentle encouragement; and my wife for her unfailingly sensible grasp of work-life matters.

1 Looking Back: Prehistoric, Ancient, and Medieval Societies

INTRODUCTION: INDUSTRIAL SOCIETY AND INDUSTRIAL SOCIOLOGY

In the last half of the eighteenth century, a unique combination of circumstances in England set in motion the Industrial Revolution. A swift reshaping of the nation's economy and society soon was underway. Before long, even distant areas of the globe were affected.

England's transformation from an agricultural society to the world's first industrialized country involved many factors. Several of these stand out (Ashton, 1969). The "enclosure movement" had pushed rural families toward urban employment; farmers lost their traditional use of the open fields when large landowners began to fence them in for sheep grazing. As canals were built, new roads laid, and existing roadbeds and surfaces greatly improved, the cost of transporting goods over long distances was greatly reduced. More metal coins were minted with the flow of gold from the New World, and private banks issued a variety of paper money. Low interest rates, from 3 to 5 percent, encouraged investment in new enterprises. The steam engine and numerous other ingenious machines were devised, replacing muscle power and proving far more productive, and agricultural innovations boosted crop yields. The expanded supply of food and improved transportation made it possible to feed the growing urban populations. Above all, the political system provided a setting in which private enterprise could flourish. Successive parliaments were composed largely of men whose interests were advanced by hands-off economic and social policies.

Due to this combination of events, small enterprises producing a customary, fixed amount for localized regional markets gave way to large firms with efficient machinery that could produce ample goods for national and international markets (Polanyi, 1957). Industrial output vastly accelerated, creating a wealthier society.

Although England was in the lead in industrial development, it did not remain the only industrialized nation or the front-runner for long. With the exception of brief Prussian campaigns against Austria and France, Western Europe experienced its longest period of peace, from the end of the Napoleonic Wars in 1815 to the outbreak of World War I in 1914. Under the umbrella of peace, a web of financial and trade relationships stimulated investment in manufacturing, especially in France and Germany.

Industrialization reached the United States rather late. In 1860 there were more slaves than factory workers, and the waterwheel, not the steam engine, powered half of the country's factories. But by the end of the century, American production nearly equaled the combined value of English, French, and German manufactured products (Gutman, 1977). At the beginning of the twentieth century, the United States was well into the transition to an industrial society. Over half of the workforce had nonfarm jobs, a proportion that would continue to grow decade by decade.

This initial look at industrialization points to the central concerns of industrial sociology—the work-related features of life in industrial society. Also of interest are the events that spawned the Industrial Revolution, conditions of life and work prior to industrialization, and what present trends might tell us about the years ahead. These topics are discussed in this book.

When it is useful to do so, we will include the information that numbers can provide. This should create no difficulty for readers, because the data are in an easily understood form. We begin with a distant time and move toward the present.

HUNTING-GATHERING SOCIETIES

Humanlike creatures (hominids) appeared first on the plains of East Africa and, about 2 million years ago, began to spread to Europe and Asia and eventually throughout the world. Remains of hominids dated nearly 4 million years old have been unearthed in Tanzania (Bower, 1992a), and more complete remains and campsites of hominids living 2.5 million years ago have been found in Kenya. These creatures were 4 feet tall, walked erect, had a brain about one-fourth the size of modern humans, and used simple stone tools to hack the flesh off the dead animals they found. About 200,000 B.C. appeared the first *Homo sapiens* (the family of modern humans). They were a foot taller than the hominids, twice as heavy, and had a brain nearly as large as today's humans. By 40,000 B.C. evolution had produced the physical characteristics of present-day humans ("Who We Were," 1991; Pfeiffer, 1977).

For 3 million years, until the beginnings of settled agriculture (8000–7000 B.C.), food-getting occupied people much of the time. By hunting, fishing, searching for berries, and digging edible roots, the earth's tiny population of perhaps 5 million people, scattered in small nomadic groups, attempted to avoid starvation. A division of labor based on age and gender arose. Lacking the stamina for hunting or foraging, old people worked at food and animal-skin preparation; children collected berries and nuts and supplied the campfire with wood. As hunting developed—from small game at first to large animals tracked on increasingly lengthy expeditions—so too did the sexual division of labor. Since pregnant or nursing women handicapped long hunts, men became the hunters, leaving the women to gather food and care for the children (Kranzberg and Gies, 1975).

For a very long time the wooden spear was the most advanced hunting weapon, until the bow and arrow came into use about 35,000 years ago. The bow gave the hunter more accuracy than was possible with a spear, and a range four times greater (Lenski and Lenski, 1982). A larger variety of materials was used for increasingly special-purpose tools— bone needles with eyes, stone saws, wood shovels and scoops (Bower, 1992b; "Dating an Ancient," 1993). Tentlike structures of leather over twigs gave shelter from the weather, and the stone lamp with animal fat for fuel and moss for a wick provided light (Lenski and Lenski, 1982).

These technical changes improved living conditions. Accidents, diseases, and malnutrition, however, made the lives of hunter-gatherers harsh and short. At least three of every four newborn babies did not survive infancy. Among those who did, the average life span was about 25 years, with only a few surviving to become old and decrepit in their thirties. With such high infant mortality and short adult lives, women had to bear five or six children just to maintain the population. Going about the daily round of tasks while almost continuously pregnant, and repeatedly exposed to the hazards of childbirth, women aged faster and died younger than men (United Nations, 1973).

The early social unit in the Stone Age was the band, which included about 25 people. Such bands eventually formed semipermanent villages of about a hundred persons. The advantages of the village were that its population was big enough to send out the larger numbers of hunters that big game required, and more men could be mustered to defend it against trespassing bands ("Seeds of Warfare," 1995). There are no indications that class distinctions existed within these villages (Childe, 1964).

The absence of social distinctions was largely due to the hand-to-mouth existence of hunter-gatherer communities. Although there were part-time specialists—individuals who were particularly adept at making snares or chipping flint for arrowheads, clever hunt leaders, priests for magical-religious rituals—food was too scarce to allow full-time activities that did not directly contribute to the food supply. Personal belongings were scant and a handicap when the dwelling place was moved. Accumulated belongings, therefore, were not available to bestow privilege. Inheritance of position also was not possible, since there was neither a full-time task to inherit nor the surplus to allow the untalented to perform tasks that affected the whole community. Scarcity thus fostered a rough equality.

This feature of early communities eventually gave way to more familiar forms. Techniques were discovered to produce a food surplus, while human ingenuity also developed intricate patterns of social organization that offered some persons privileged access to the surplus. Aside from a few small communities, the skewed distribution of societies' goods is everywhere evident. Despite egalitarian ideologies and even revolutions, inequality remains after the dust has settled. This persistent characteristic of social life became visible in the late Stone Age, or the Neolithic period.

THE AGRICULTURAL REVOLUTION

Archeologists refer to the period from 8000 to 3000 B.C. as the Neolithic or New Stone Age. Although the Neolithic period was only an instant in the 2 million years of the Stone Age, revolutionary changes were compressed into it. The descendants of nomadic peoples became sedentary. Earlier means of survival by hunting and gathering faded as permanent settlements were built and new patterns of existence based on agriculture were fashioned.

Agriculture developed independently in several places—Mesoamerica (Mexico to Peru), Southeast Asia, and the Fertile Crescent—and spread from these areas. The earliest agricultural region, the Fertile Crescent, extends from the eastern shore of the Mediterranean to the Persian Gulf, arcing across present-day Turkey, Israel, and Syria to Iraq and Iran. In prehistoric times this terrain flourished with game and fields of wild cereal grasses. From about 9000 to 6000 B.C., hunting and harvesting wild grasses were combined with agriculture. Then, from 6000 to 5000

B.C., the yield from farming became the main food source. In addition to wheat and barley, lentils and peas were domesticated, as were sheep, pigs, and cattle (Braidwood and Dyson, 1968; "Mesopotamia," 1981). Though there is no sure way to know, women's knowledge of plants, gained from millennia of collecting them, suggests that the earliest sowers of seed and harvesters were women, whereas men, accustomed to the hunt, domesticated animals and herded them (Childe, 1964). With permanent settlements came more weatherproof shelters. Sun-baked clay slabs and bricks provided materials for houses, some of which were two-storied with a basement for food storage. Homes such as this were built in the villages of the Fertile Crescent some 9,000 years ago, complete with separate rooms, hinged doors, and porthole windows (Pfeiffer, 1977).

Neolithic villages typically contained perhaps 20 to 25 houses, although some became much larger, such as the town of Jericho, which had 2,000 to 3,000 inhabitants in 7000 B.C. Most families were self-sufficient, making whatever they used. In the larger Neolithic towns, however, occupational specialization was advancing. Small workshops of craftsmen made weapons, pottery, bone tools, and woven cloth. Towns as large as Jericho were centers of trade. The surrounding farmers and herdsmen brought their produce and livestock to barter for goods, and merchants from distant places brought obsidian (highly prized for weapons) from Asia and cowrie shells (an early form of money) from the Red Sea region to exchange for the town's products (Lenski and Lenski, 1982). The existence of surplus food had triggered far-reaching changes, although the excess was individually quite small. A rough estimate is that between 80 and 100 people doing farming and herding could support one town dweller (Braidwood and Dyson, 1968).

The organization of early Neolithic towns and villages is unclear, but there is little evidence of distinctions in rank among the inhabitants. Warfare was uncommon, as indicated by the absence of walls around most settlements and the lack of battle weapons in men's graves. In the later Neolithic period, however, fortified walls surrounded towns, and daggers or battle axes have been found in the graves of nearly all adult males (Lenski and Lenski, 1982). The growing wealth of the towns and their nearby herds of cattle were apparently irresistible temptations to plunder. In the later Neolithic period, also, bronze was used for weapons, offering an inducement to warriors who had metal weapons to attack settlements defended with less sturdy arms. War had become a brutish, all-or-nothing undertaking. As a prelude to carrying off their booty, the victors usually slaughtered all survivors. In the coming period, when great empires were built, the practice grew of sparing the vanquished inhabitants to be sold as slaves or to provide a source of taxes.

CITY-STATES AND EMPIRES: THE EMERGENCE OF ELITES

By the dawn of the Bronze Age 5,000 years ago, a new form of social organization was in place. Urban-based warlords, commanding warriors equipped with bronze weapons, had subdued agriculturalists still using stone weapons. Warlords, officials, and priests emerged as a privileged governing class supported by military power and religious beliefs. This new form of social organization first appeared in the Sumerian city-states and Egypt.

Sumerian City-States

Along the banks and tributaries of the Tigris and Euphrates rivers are scattered the traces of ancient, prosperous cities in Sumeria (present-day Iraq). These cities, the world's first urban-centered power hubs, dominated the Fertile Crescent. Ur in 3000 B.C. had a population of at least 24,000; Uruk had 20,000; Umma, 16,000. Each densely populated city was surrounded by a brick wall enclosing a palace, temple, granaries, workshops, and houses. With intensive cultivation and city-directed irrigation, the neighboring countryside was able to supply the city's food. Materials not locally available were imported: copper from the Persian Gulf region, tin from Iran, timber from the mountains to the northeast (Childe, 1964).

Ur, Umma, and other large cities were administrative centers that controlled the surrounding farmland and organized the construction and upkeep of the water-control devices (canals, reservoirs, dams) that irrigated the land.[1] Each city and its countryside constituted a small kingdom, a city-state. What made this possible was that by the time these city-states had developed in the beginning of the Bronze Age (3000 to 1000 B.C.), several innovations had made agriculture more productive, the transport of goods over long distances easier, and administrative control more effective.

Agriculture's long dependence on the hoe gave way to the wooden plow pulled by oxen. Because it digs deeper, a plow buries weeds, adding nutrients to the soil. Harnessing oxen not only opened larger land areas to cultivation, but the manure collected from their stalls pro-

---

[1]The classic study of the origin of the political state is Karl Wittfogel's *Oriental Despotism* (1957). Noting the autocratic regimes that arose in Sumeria, Egypt, India, and China, Wittfogel reasoned that mass labor was required to construct and maintain their elaborate irrigation systems; and since mass labor needed leadership and discipline, the centralized political state with its bureaucratic apparatus emerged in response to the need for administrative control. Others look to warfare as an explanation of the origin of the state (Carneiro, 1970).

vided fertilizer. When these improvements were combined with irrigation, agricultural yields sharply rose.

Food produced in the countryside somehow had to be transported to
the cities. Using wind power, small boats with sails provided one means
of transport (Childe, 1964), but the old techniques of dragging goods on
sledges or slung between poles were too slow and not well adapted to
moving large quantities. This difficulty was overcome by the invention of
the wheel; both two- and four-wheeled carts, pulled by oxen, donkeys, or
horses, were put into use. One practice with oxen, however, limited the
load a horse or donkey could pull. The harness used for oxen passed
across their shoulders and throats so that they pushed against it with
their broad shoulders. Since the same harness was used for horses and
donkeys, who do not have broad shoulders, they often nearly choked
themselves when they pulled the carts. Not until the ninth century A.D.
was the shoulder harness invented (Braudel, 1967).

Organized around king and temple, a Sumerian city-state was a
theocracy (Linton, 1955). Each city housed its chief god in a large temple
and provided the diety with priestly servants, a wife, and numerous
concubines. The king's authority was derived from two sources: He
commanded a well-equipped and highly trained army, and he was the
intermediary between the city's god and the city-state's inhabitants
(Childe, 1964). The fusion of military might and religious belief gave
the ruler awesome power.

All land belonged in principle to the city's god. To use the land, peasants paid to the temple a rent of 10 percent of everything they produced.
This supplied food for the temple's inhabitants; to provide for their
other needs, hundreds of craftsmen were employed in the temple workshops. In order to pay the artisans in pieces of silver and copper, which
served as money, temple prostitutes sold their services to devout visitors, and priests predicted the future and conducted funerals.

As the representative of the city's deity, the king claimed hundreds of
acres of land. The taxes from it (paid in kind) were used for the upkeep
of the king's household and army. Most of the booty from military campaigns also went to the king. The enormous income required to sustain
a royal household was indicated by the discovery of a palace in Ebla,
Syria. Nearly 12,000 persons served this palace when it was at its prime
in 2500 B.C. (LaFay, 1978).

Although in theory peasants paid rent to the city's god, the rent col-
lectors were the priests. Keeping detailed records of all debts, revenues,
and expenditures presented a formidable task. Around 3000 B.C. writing
developed to cope with this administrative obligation. First was picture
writing or hieroglyphics (Derber, Schwartz, and Magrass, 1990). This
was simplified by the Sumerian priests into a system of symbols to rep-

resent spoken syllables; by combining these symbols, compound sounds could be written. This writing is called *cuneiform* because a wedge-shaped stylus was used to make impressions on clay tablets. (The cuneiform tablets were customarily baked, thus preserving them for archeologists.) Schools were opened in temples to teach priestly scribes writing and some mathematics, which was developed about the same time as writing and largely for the same purposes.

Scribes were much in demand as temple record keepers and for the king's growing bureaucracy. In the scores of villages and towns in a city-state's domain, officials organized the irrigation work, dispensed justice, and collected taxes, while numerous other officials were responsible for administering the royal household and army. Administration had become such a complex affair that every official had a staff of scribes (Childe, 1964).

The invention of writing provided a superb tool for managing a society in which everyone had a legally defined station in life. Standards of living roughly corresponded to social position, and the legal system reinforced it. For instance, injury to a state official, soldier, or priest was far more severely punished than a similar injury to an artisan or other commoner (shopkeeper, merchant, farmer). If a slave were injured, no one was physically punished for it, although the owner received financial compensation for damage to his property (Linton, 1955). It is doubtful that the centralized bureaucracies that maintained these arrangements could have emerged without the assistance of writing.

The era of independent city-states did not last in Sumeria. Border skirmishes between neighboring kingdoms erupted into military campaigns of conquest. One city-state after the other fell to the king of Uruk, until, in 2500 B.C., he governed an empire extending over all of Sumeria. And so it went. As a dynasty weakened, the country fragmented; kings of cities fought until one emerged victorious and reunited the empire.

The spoils of victory were great indeed. Possessing enormous wealth, thousands of servants, winter and summer palaces, an emperor could gratify almost every desire except to remain in power. The empire of Sumeria abruptly ended when it was invaded by Alexander the Great's Macedonian army in the fourth century B.C. Certainly, for the great majority of people, most of whom were peasants, the rise and fall of rulers did not change their lives. The divisions remained between slaves, commoners, and the governing class of hereditary aristocrats.

Alexander's troops were armed with iron weapons, as were the opposing forces. For several hundred years iron making had been a carefully guarded secret of the Hittites in Asia Minor (now Turkey). When the Hittite empire collapsed in 1200 B.C., knowledge of iron making spread to other peoples. The scarcity of iron, as well as its great advantage over bronze in weapons, initially made iron objects exported by the Hittites more valuable than gold or silver. After the secret technique of iron making had been disclosed, iron weapons became widely used, and by 800 B.C. tools and plowshares were also being made of this metal. Two discoveries had further added to the usefulness of iron: alternately heating and cooling the iron to give it greater strength, and adding carbon to produce steel. Stronger and more flexible than bronze, and holding a sharp edge longer, iron was a very useful metal.

State Proprietorship in Egypt

Nearly everyone lived close to the level of subsistence in agriculturally based societies. The exceptions were the aristocracy and upper tier of priests and those who defended the society as soldiers or served its elite as artisans and merchants. In order to maintain these groups, peasants had to provide rents, taxes, and obligatory labor on roads, irrigation works, or (as in Egypt) pyramids.

These arrangements are explained by the "proprietary theory of the state," a point of view shared by power holders in agricultural societies (Lenski, 1966). In this perspective, the state is the personal property of its "owner" and can be inherited by the ruler's heirs. The state can be used for personal advantage, and portions of the land can be assigned to favored persons.

Among the most extreme cases of state proprietorship was ancient Egypt. In Sumeria, as we saw, a king exercised power as the intermediary to a god. But upon the coronation of an Egyptian king (pharaoh), he *became* a god.

The prosperity of the country depended on the pharaoh's spiritual potency, which was maximized by purity of the royal blood. To ensure this, the pharaohs customarily married their own sisters. The pharaoh's palace was constructed in the form of a temple, since he was the physical embodiment of a god. It was believed that even after his death, the well-being of the country was influenced by the pharaoh's anger or good will in the afterlife.

Egypt was unified about 2900 B.C. and fell to Alexander just before his conquest of Sumeria. Thus, for nearly 3,000 years, pharaohs were the absolute rulers of the country. All land was the pharaoh's property, and the surplus Egypt produced went into the royal granaries, while gold from the state's mines filled the pharaoh's treasuries.

All peasants were initially serfs, bound to the royal household, temple, or noble's land they cultivated. About 2000 B.C. the serfs were freed, but they could not actually leave because no other land was available.

Whether serf or free, peasants were obliged to pay taxes (in kind) on all crops and rent to the owner of the land.

To administer taxes, a large bureaucratic apparatus was required. Priests used the hieroglyphic form of writing[2] that was taught along with mathematics to the temple-trained scribes who served as bureaucratic officials. Periodically, the government took a census. The information went to district offices that maintained records detailing land size, types of crops, and probable yields. This supplied the basis for determining the percentage of the crop to be delivered to the government as tax. Another set of officials annually issued regulations that specified when and what to plant (Jacoby, 1973).

The distribution of state revenues was closely tied to rank in the government. From local administrative centers, all officials received graded incomes in the form of a daily food ration of loaves of bread, cuts of meat, and jugs of beer. These were prepared in the bakery, kitchens, and brewery operated by the state in each center. For exceptional service, officials were rewarded with land grants and bonuses; gold and copper rings served as money. Selected from the hereditary nobility, some officials were awarded the high honor of appointment to the pharaoh's palace, where they would share its luxurious lifestyle.

Pyramid Building and Economic Decline

Though immense resources were required to live in such a grand style, it was manageable through the tax system and the government's monopoly on gold mining. Economic strain, however, was caused by the curious practice (to the modern mind) of pyramid building. When the pharaoh was crowned, he soon began to prepare for his death by having a pyramid raised. This was an extremely important undertaking. Because the pyramid would house the pharaoh's sacred corpse, it must be protected for his afterlife as a god. The mummy was therefore placed in an impenetrable inner room. Anything the pharaoh might need must be provided: servants (in the form of small statues), a boat, gold, prized possessions. Priests dedicated to the service of the pharaoh brought offerings of food to his mausoleum for generations. These practices were expected to guarantee the pharaoh a satisfactory afterlife and thus assure the country's prosperity.

---

[2]Hieroglyphic and cuneiform writing both require the memorization of hundreds of signs. Much easier to learn are symbols for the most elemental sounds of speech, a form of script invented in Syria around 1500 B.C. Within a century, an alphabet of 31 characters was being employed. Around the same time there was an early version of the Phoenician alphabet, from which the alphabet we use descended by way of Greece and Rome ("New Levant," 1981).

A master builder, selected by the pharaoh, was responsible for the pyramid's construction. Quarrying, hauling, shaping, and placing the stones were done by peasants as a compulsory duty in the season when the Nile flooded and farmwork was impossible. A variety of craftsmen were involved— certainly artists (to decorate) and masons and carpenters, who were provided with metal tools for their work. The Great Pyramid of Cheops (about 2600 B.C.) illustrates the staggering amount of labor consumed by pyramid building. This pyramid contains 2.3 million limestone blocks, each weighing over two tons. Construction spanned 20 years, with a labor force of 100,000 men during the project. Every worker was housed, fed, and clothed from the pharaoh's revenues ("New Levant," 1981; Roberts, 1995).

Working without wheel or pulley, human and animal power was used to move the great stones by laying greased boards and sliding the stones forward. The stones were cut from rock by drilling along the grain, inserting wedges of wood, and then soaking the wood with water to swell it enough to crack the rock. When this failed, wooden wedges were inserted and heated with fire, then doused with cold water to crack the rock. The rough blocks were then shaped with bronze-toothed saws and hauled into place. The stones fit so perfectly that no mortar was needed to hold them together.

Reports by overseers' scribes offer a glimpse of conditions of work on the pyramids. Fortunately for the laborers, they were not considered expendable. A report on a quarry team, for instance, notes that not a man or mule was lost. Another report details the food and clothing provided to laborers: "4 lbs. bread, 2 bundles of vegetables and a roast of meat daily, and a clean linen garment twice a month" (Kranzberg and Gies, 1975, p. 50).

Visitors to Egypt were dazzled by its display of prosperity, but the glitter was superficial. Taxes had stifled the productive potential of the country: Too much had been taken out of the economy, and too little was left. Except when the producers were directly employed by a pharaoh, noble, or temple, they could afford only Neolithic equipment of copper or stone and wood. Egyptian craftsmen were excellent—colored glass (used for beads and inlays) had been discovered, wood veneering was highly developed, and all the various wood joints known today were used by cabinet makers. Jewelers made objects of gold and electrum (a natural alloy of gold and silver) which are still copied, and physicians had remedies to remove wrinkles or darken gray hair (Linton, 1955). The problem was that the market for these products and services was mainly a small governing circle of royal officials, the hereditary aristocracy, and the upper ranks of priests.

Egypt was well organized to squeeze maximum revenues from tax-payers for the comfort of its rulers. But Egypt's military forces were on occasion disastrously unreliable. With only slight resistance, Egypt fell to Alexander the Great in 332 B.C.; 300 years later, Greek rule ended and Rome's began. Egypt then served as a source of wheat for the Roman Empire. The conditions of peasants' lives were no better than before, and sometimes worse. If Rome's military campaigns required more than the usual supplies of grain, the tax (in kind) on peasants was steeply increased.

The Roman Empire

After gaining control of Egypt, the armies of Rome marched to further conquests. Penetrating even into Britain, the empire became the largest that had ever existed in the Western world. To maintain the armies required enormous revenues, obtained from Roman citizens and the conquered territories. A sales tax and a tax on inheritance were collected, as well as customs duties and a land tax. The land tax was the agriculturalists' burden and supplied the largest share of the empire's taxes, although the majority of farms were small and provided little more than subsistence (Antonio, 1979).

Roman might imposed peace on the area under its domination. Trade flourished inside the empire and between it and distant places (Childe, 1964). Pottery, glassware, and textiles were manufactured and sold in the empire; from China and India came luxuries for the wealthy—dancing girls, parrots, silks, perfumes, drugs. Safe travel on paved roads and on the Mediterranean Sea encouraged the expansion of trade. But wealth was highly concentrated. The purchasing power of the vast majority of people was quite low because free craftsmen and laborers were in competition with slave labor. Workshop staffs were one-third to one-half free men, with the rest slaves or ex-slaves.

A larger textile manufacturer might employ 25 weavers, a pottery-making shop perhaps 10 to 14 artisans. Most commonly, a shop was operated by the craftsman-owner, assisted by a hired worker or slave who performed the routine preparatory tasks. Except for workshops that supplied military needs or materials such as bricks or tiles, manufacturing was a small-scale affair. The shops, though, were highly specialized. Pottery makers specialized in producing cooking pots, jars, goblets, or large urns; separate woodworking shops made couches, chests, or caskets.

Housing patterns followed craft lines. Craftsmen with a particular skill lived in one section of the city or along a certain street. The specialized crafts formed guilds that held religious services for their members and collected money for sick members or their burials. (These early organizations were forerunners of both the guilds in the Middle Ages and modern labor unions.)

The craft guild was an important institution in Rome's attempt to stabilize the level of production. Output had fallen when violent disorders prompted urban workers to leave their occupations and migrate to the countryside. In the third century, by order of the emperor, guild members were forbidden to leave their guilds, and their sons had to remain in the families' occupations (Damus, 1968).

At the height of Rome's power, architects and builders were busy with the construction of roads, aqueducts, public baths, theaters, and colosseums. Though the mass of people benefited from these amenities, in other respects life was grim. Unemployment was so high that a large portion of the population depended on the free grain supplied by the government. To further win the people's approval, spectacular shows were presented in the colosseums and theaters. The brutality of the times is revealed in these "entertainments." The emperor Trajan, for instance, celebrated his victories by providing the populace with 10,000 captives fighting to the death in the Colosseum. In the theaters, if the script called for a torture scene, a criminal was put to death (Damus, 1968).

Most people lived poorly, although the lives of some were comfortable. The small middle class, consisting of merchants and owners of larger workshops, was relatively well-off, while the Roman aristocracy enjoyed a regal standard of living. As members of the governing class in a huge empire, they filled the top administrative offices and had ample opportunities to accept bribes. The nobility also owned spacious farms which brought large incomes.

The extensive estates (called *latifundia*) were operated throughout the sprawling empire on a commercial basis for the benefit of the aristocratic owners. Typically, overseers managed the estates (Kranzberg and Gies, 1975). The owners were mostly absent, enjoying the banquets, baths, and entertainments of urban life or engaged in the few activities that were considered appropriate to the Roman elite. To the high-born Romans (the Sumerian, Greek, and Egyptian aristocracies had felt much the same), "The most noble of all men was the man who had enough wealth in landed property, who had no occupation at all, and who could devote himself to politics and war, two activities associated with power, influence, and prestige rather than with work or occupation" (Applebaum, 1992, p. 97).

Using slaves at first and later a mix of slaves and tenant farmers for labor, the latifundia in an area specialized in raising grapes, olives, or livestock. Though in a few places the waterwheel, used for grinding grain, began to appear, for the most part there was little change in agriculture. The Romans were content to use traditional methods of farming and other work.

Over time, large farms held a growing share of the farmland. Civil wars led to the abandonment of many small farms, creating unused land. Imperial decrees directed landowners to cultivate idle fields adjoining theirs. As anarchy ravaged the countryside, more farmers left their small plots. Those who remained were assessed heavier taxes to compensate for the government's decreasing revenues, which further encouraged farmers to leave and join the ranks of tenant farmers under large landowners.

The latifundia initially depended on urban industry. Clothes, bricks, and wooden and metal objects were bought in town, and urban craftsmen were hired for repair work. Though trade in difficult-to-make items—glassware, swords, armor—never entirely stopped, the estates increasingly met their own needs (Applebaum, 1992).

Tenant farmers received seed and equipment from the landlord. In return, the farmers paid rent in kind and provided whatever labor services the estate might require. Moreover, since the government was increasingly unable to operate a judicial system within the empire, the landlord determined justice among disputing tenants. In this flow of events, aristocratic landowners' mansions were on the way to becoming castles. Landlords would be transformed into armor-clad knights, and tenant farmers would become serfs.

THE MIDDLE AGES

The Roman Empire disintegrated soon after the Huns pushed into Europe from their homeland in Mongolia. The Hun migration set to flight Germanic tribes, some of which fled south into Italy with the Huns close behind. The government of Rome, unable to withstand the large numbers and fierce combativeness of the invaders, totally collapsed in the late 400s. A Hun chieftain dominated Rome, and the western part of the Roman Empire was finished. The eastern part—the Byzantine Empire—managed to survive into the middle of the fifteenth century, but the collapse of the Roman Empire marked Europe's entry into the Middle Ages. The manorial system provided the economic foundation of the Middle Ages; the feudal system, with its hierarchy of lords, clergy, and serfs, supplied the political framework.

The Manorial System

Urban life requires the movement of food to cities and the transport of wares to and from cities. Usable roads and water routes are essential, and they are provided by effective governments. With the fall of the Roman Empire, trade withered as roads deteriorated, bandits preyed on travelers, and pirates hunted traders on the Mediterranean Sea. Government officials were unable to halt the slide toward chaos. The self-contained manorial form of economy was the result.

A manor typically included a village, fields, pasture, woodland, and the landholder's fortified residence (castle) ringed by a wall and sometimes a moat, which also enclosed a building for grain storage and perhaps a chapel. Besides the landowner, his family, some men-at-arms, and possibly a priest, the manor was populated by serfs. The status was permanent: The serfs, their families and their descendants were "tied to the soil."

Half the manor's farmland was usually the lord's; the other half was used by the serfs. They also cultivated the lord's portion for two or three days a week, and the yield went to him. The serfs, additionally, constructed and repaired the estate's roads, walls, buildings, and equipment and made clothes for the manorial community (Applebaum, 1992). Moreover, serfs had to pay (in kind) for using the lord's grain mill, wine press, and bread ovens. A portion of flour, for instance, was deducted from each sack milled. After all this, not much was left to sustain the serfs. If things went well, if no drought, crop failure, or war came along, serfs lived on little more than 1,600 calories per day (Wolf, 1966).[3]

The Feudal System

The estates were parts of larger political alliances. Weak landlords lost their estates to more powerful lords or swore loyalty to them. Land granted by a lord was a *fief;* the fief holder was the lord's vassal and was pledged to military service when required by his overlord. A fief could be further subdivided, limited only by the amount of land required to support a fully equipped knight. This arrangement linked aristocratic landholders into a hierarchy of military obligations. At first precariously and then firmly, monarchs occupied the tips of these regional pyramids.

The lengthy training, discipline, and wealth demanded for combat forged the knights into a self-conscious class of nobles who disdained ordinary work and had contempt for those who did not bear arms. Damus (1968) notes that "During the feudal period, the principal business of those who ruled was war.... The vassal and the knights he owed his lord must be ready to fight, and they must know how to fight. So

---

[3]About 3,000 calories a day is currently considered adequate for a physically hard-working man. Into the 1800s, the great majority of people everywhere existed on at least a third fewer calories (Braudel, 1973).

from boyhood this class began preparing itself for its future role" (p. 303). With the serfs forbidden to bear arms, they were helpless to resist the nobles' demands for labor on their terms. Most members of the rural population—which included almost everyone—were serfs; among the rest were a few freemen, churchmen, and the tiny governing class of nobles, no more than 1 percent of the whole population (Manchester, 1993).

The knights engaged in endless bloody quarrels sparked by territorial disputes or revenge. Starting in the last years of the eleventh century, and for the next 200 years, Europe was spared considerable bloodshed when the knights accepted the Church's call to undertake the Crusades and expel the Moslems from the Holy Land. The promise of salvation, and the possibility of booty, amplified the call to holy war (Finucane, 1983). While the lord was gone, the knight's wife usually took over supervision of the estate. According to Adams and others (1990), "The lady of the manor…had to deal with the management of acres of land, crops, animals, and property; … legal arguments, fights, riots and even armed attacks" (pp. 6–8). The Church attempted to establish rules of conduct to lessen the nobles' combativeness, but with little success.

Agricultural Innovations

Despite the turbulent conditions, a number of important innovations greatly increased the level of production in the manorial system.

The heavy wheeled plow so thoroughly split earth clods that crossplowing was eliminated. After the horseshoe and padded horsecollar were invented, plodding oxen gave way to much faster draft horses for plowing. The greatest agricultural innovation of the Middle Ages was the three-field system of crop rotation. Under the older two-field plan, half the usable land was planted each year while the other half remained idle. With the three-field system, the arable land was divided into thirds, keeping only one-third of the land idle, or fallow. The actual gain, however, was substantially greater because planted land was plowed once, fallow land twice. The result was one-third more cropland with less plowing (White, 1962).

By the eleventh century, use of these techniques was widespread, creating an agricultural system which supported a larger population. About this time, too, water mills were becoming common. Within another hundred years, the windmill was adopted for areas where water was sluggish or not readily available. Power from wind and water was used to hammer iron, drive saws, crush ore, polish armor, grind grain for bread, and even to launder clothes.

The medieval interest in harnessing nature's power was intense, and mechanisms to do so more effectively, including complex gears and the crank (to connect reciprocating and rotary motion), were devised. Gunpowder, a new source of energy to drive such mechanisms, was available in Europe in the 1400s. Gunpowder for artillery was militarily important, but equally significant was the cannon's construction as a one-cylinder internal combustion engine using the energy of expanding gases. Modern motors of this type are based on the same principle (White, 1962).

The Guild System in Towns

The manor represents the rural, agricultural core of the Middle Ages. Guilds developed with the revival of towns. Though the manor remained the center of existence for the vast majority of people, its self-containment gradually lessened as money and trade began to circulate.

After a 500-year gap, urban life began to revive around the walls of castles, as well as in ecclesiastical centers that sheltered a cathedral, one or two monasteries, and the residences of church officials. In the eleventh century a few traders settled in these rudimentary towns; more soon followed. In the old order of knights, clergy, and serfs, merchants were a strange breed of man, free from the authority of a lord and profit-minded. Their origins are unclear; most were probably the runaway children of serfs, but they were treated as free men. As their numbers swelled, a new social segment, the bourgeoisie, came into being.

The merchants' commercial activities were a magnet that attracted artisans of every kind to the expanding towns. Bakers, brewers, shoemakers, and tailors practiced their trades; others worked up the raw material imported by the merchants. These wares further stimulated export trade. In Flanders (western Belgium) wool weavers came to the towns. The Flemish cloth trade quickly became the most flourishing industry of Europe and remained so until the end of the Middle Ages (Pirenne, 1955). The nobility enjoyed access to many kinds of products and benefited from taxes on merchants and artisans.

Although the aristocracy suffered some loss of local authority, the advantages of commerce led many nobles to offer privileges and immunities to merchants to attract them. Eventually, the bourgeoisie developed forms of urban government that were wholly independent of the high-born (except for taxes). The aristocracy retained its traditional privilege and jurisdiction in the still largely agricultural society of the Middle Ages, but the old rural order was changing. A money economy was developing. Peasants sold their produce on local markets; the lord used his rent money for urban goods. Beginning in the twelfth century, serfs could gain their freedom from lords by purchasing it. The serf, now a peasant, paid a money rent to the lord for use of a parcel of land, although the peasant was still obliged to work on the owner's fields several days a week. However, the labor duty the peasant had performed for the castle—repair of roads, construction of bridges and moats, spinning, weaving, blacksmithing—was now done by hired hands. As before, the peasant paid a tithe to the church and fees to the lord for use of the grain mill, wine press, and bread ovens. When the noble's son was knighted or his daughter married, the peasants made a payment; in the event the lord was captured, part of the ransom was paid by the peasants (Tuchman, 1978). The local seigneur was still the master of his manor, while new wealth was generated amidst urban life.

From the twelfth through the fifteenth centuries, urban commercial activities were dominated by merchant and craft guilds. Their aim was the regulation of business activities within an area, to the exclusion of outsiders. The right to organize was granted by a charter obtained from a local seigneur or ecclesiastical lord. A new member paid an entrance fee and was asked to take an oath of loyalty to the guild, promising to obey its laws and officers and not to divulge trade secrets. Guild participants were required to attend members' funerals and share expenses. On feast days, members attended devotional services in a chapel supported by the guild. Each guild enforced its rules through a guild court.

Merchant guilds were concerned with buying and selling imported goods; craft guilds were focused on production. Merchant guilds specified the selling place of items (usually the guildhall or marketplace), restricted the hours during which sales could be made, and regulated who might buy, often excluding people from other communities. They could forbid the sale of nonmembers' wares and had the important privilege of making a first offer on cargoes brought to certain ports (Davis, 1961). Dealing in marble, herring, wool, grains, and gold, the merchant guilds were the main suppliers of such desirable goods, at a time when the circulation of money was increasing. Successful merchants became very wealthy and politically powerful in urban government.

Craft guilds were organized around craftsmen with specific skills, such as ribbon and lace makers, weavers, tailors, carpenters, brewers, bakers, shoemakers, and launderers. Within the craft guilds there was further specialization. One carpenter made furniture, another built houses, a third did wood carving; one baker's shop sold white bread, another brown bread. Spreading the work to more people was the intention and the result. Unlike merchant guilds, craft guilds included employers (masters) and employees (journeymen and apprentices) in their memberships. Some women, though many fewer than men, were guild members. Both men and women were apprentices, and both women and men were masters who took apprentices. Sometimes wives helped their husbands in their crafts, and some women operated their own businesses as independent members of a craft guild (Adams et al., 1990).

The master craftsman or woman owned a shop, directed the work of apprentices and journeymen, and sold the finished products. An apprentice was a young person whom a master had contracted (for a fee) to train for a period of three to seven years. The master provided the apprentice with a bed, food, clothes, and perhaps a little spending money. The relationship was broad, including perhaps a bit of schooling and definitely a good deal of discipline. On completion of training, the apprentice became a journeyman, a fully qualified artisan who could become a master by producing a "masterpiece" acceptable to guild officials.

Craft guilds regulated hours of work, the tools and materials that could be used, and the quality and price of products. According to guild rules, working at night, on Saturday afternoons, and on church feast days was everywhere prohibited. Lorimers (makers of riding equipment) specified that no cast iron should be used in making bridles and prohibited the making of saddlebows except with specified woods. Beef was not to be baked in pies and sold as venison, and rabbits were not to be baked in pies at all. Cap makers were not to dye white or grey wool black, since the color would be taken out by rain. Baskets for fish were to be of proper size, made to contain only one kind of fish and not to be filled with better fish on top than below (Davis, 1961).

For a seller to receive more than the official price for a product was a punishable offense. If poor work was suspected, guild officers had the authority to search the houses of members for evidence. To ease the burdens of control, guild members were usually required to live in the same neighborhood, and craftsmen were required to put a mark on each article and leave a copy of the mark with the guild. Serious and repeated offenses could result in imprisonment if fines and confiscation of goods had failed to make the point.

Craft guilds succeeded in enforcing their regulations aimed at stable employment for members and protection of buyers against overpriced, shoddy products. Signs of decay nevertheless became visible in the 1500s. Advancement had become increasingly difficult for journeymen. The fee for attaining master rank was so costly that some towns intervened, thereby weakening the autonomy of guilds. And guilds became fragmented when prosperous masters set themselves apart from others by adopting special clothing that exhibited their status. More important, the assembly, in which all guild members had a vote, came to be dominated by the wealthiest masters, essentially putting control of the guilds in their hands. The concerns of the ordinary participants—control of work processes to spread the work around—conflicted with the prosperous masters' interests in cheaper and speedier production for an expanding market. The medieval notion of the "just price" (an amount that returned to the artisan the cost of production plus a traditional, reasonable gain) was giving way to open-ended profit, limited only by what buyers are willing to pay.

As craft guilds declined, some continued, though weakened, while others were absorbed by merchant guilds or became dependent on merchants who exported their goods. Merchant guilds and individual traders were seeking new ways to take advantage of the expanding commercial opportunities offered in the sixteenth century. With France and England in the lead, monarchies were strong enough to provide relatively safe roads for the business traveler; sea transport, though riskier, was often worth the gamble because it was less costly. The merchant now could see the possibility of handsome profits, but a new form of production was needed.

The Putting-Out System

In the Middle Ages various products were manufactured in particular regions for export to widely dispersed markets. Nuremberg and Toledo produced arms and armor; Cordova made shoes and leather goods; Poitiers and Limoges were famous for tapestries and rugs, Venice for mirrors and glasswares, Seville for silk cloth (Kranzberg and Gies, 1975). Although the guild system kept its hold on such products, merchants determined prices and profit levels. As the vital link between producers and markets, merchants were admirably situated in the export trade, but the small-shop production of the guilds could not keep up with the growing demand for some commodities. The merchant-entrepreneur's solution was variously called the putting-out system, cottage industry, or domestic system.

While putting-out was used to supply local markets with goods such as clothes, lace, hats, cutlery, and nails, it reached its peak in the making of wool cloth (Braverman, 1974). From the fifteenth to the eighteenth centuries, this most-flourishing export was supplied by merchants through putting-out arrangements in England and Flanders, the sources of the best raw material. The wool had to be combed to set the fibers parallel and remove undesirable fibers, spun into yarn, woven, fulled by cleaning and compacting, and finally smoothed and dyed. The steps in the procedure were very old. Although peasants wore itchy, coarse material that was neither fulled nor dyed, the complete process produced a comfortable cloth.[4] What was new in putting-out was the system of production.

The merchant-entrepreneur hired workers for the final stages of manufacturing, fulling, and dyeing the cloth, either in a specialist's small shop or the merchant's own establishment. The steps of combing, spinning, and weaving were done in peasants' homes. The merchant or his agent distributed (put out) raw wool to a number of cottages, collected the yarn after a time, and then delivered it to other cottages for weaving. For each transaction the price was set by the merchant. The arrangement was workable, though clumsy. To recruit people, the merchant went from cottage to cottage until enough workers were found. Between the merchant's establishment and his spinners' and weavers' homes, a distance of 15 or 20 miles was not unusual (Mantoux, 1961).

The workers continued to earn part of their living from farming, but in winter they turned to spinning and weaving for extra income. The home that the work was done in was often a one-room cottage serving as workshop, kitchen, and bedroom. Windows were few and narrow, with movable wooden shutters against storms, and perhaps oiled paper to let in light. A fireplace gave heat, but barely a few feet away.[5]

While the children combed the fleece, the peasant or his wife sat at the spinning wheel; among weavers, both men and women operated the hand looms. If the children were old enough, they too spun or wove. Considering the dawn-to-dusk hours worked by so many family members, the economic returns were quite skimpy. Although they worked in familiar surroundings and were not bound to specific work hours and rules set by an outsider (as in the factory system), cottage industry was dreary and grim for the peasant families.

In years of poor harvest peasants had to borrow money. The most likely source was the merchant, and he was usually willing. Security was demanded for the loan; spinning wheel and loom provided it. From the seventeenth into the eighteenth centuries, more often than not the peasant permanently lost his tools. Unable to get out of debt, he rented tools from the merchant (Mantoux, 1961).

Here and there a merchant would collect 10 or 12 workers and equipment in his own workshop, while also using workers in their own homes. This mix of old and new was practiced in woolen-goods manufacturing despite the advantages of centralized production. Compared to

---

[4]Severe skin afflictions were widespread among medieval peasants. Kranzberg and Gies (1975) note that these ailments resulted from wearing coarse wool cloth.

[5]Cold rooms were common into the 1700s, when changes in fireplace and chimney design finally brought relief (Braudel, 1973). An observer in the early 1700s remarked on cold so intense in the palace at Versailles that liquids froze and shattered bottles (Saint-Simon, 1964, p. 44).

carting material between widely scattered cottages, transportation costs were drastically cut by bringing employees into a factory. Once there, moreover, it was easier to supervise them to assure consistent product quality, waste and loss of material were more controllable, and the division of labor was in the owner's hands.

In the first half of the 1700s, England's largest export was wool cloth, partly from factories. Industrialization was speeded by developments in another branch of the textile industry, cotton cloth. It, too, had been produced by putting-out arrangements, though only in relatively small quantities for local markets. By the end of the century, cotton cloth had displaced wool as the primary export. Because of the nature of the materials, the making of cotton cloth was more readily mechanized, and a number of mechanical inventions changed the methods and location of work. Later generations called this reshaping of production the Industrial Revolution.

SUMMARY

Cities arose within a few millennia after hunter-gatherer nomads had settled in villages and planted crops. About 3000 B.C. in Sumeria and Egypt, the division of society into rulers and ruled had swiftly occurred when agriculture provided the surplus food to support urban, administrative centers. No matter who held power, peasants' lives were little changed. Existing close to the level of subsistence, labor and taxes were their lot.

Rome governed a huge empire for several hundred years. When the empire crumbled in the late 400s, trade withered and the manorial system of production took hold. The estate of the Middle Ages was by necessity self-reliant; serfs carried out the labor necessary for sustaining the manor's inhabitants.

Trade began to revive in the eleventh century. Merchants settled outside the walls of castles and in ecclesiastical cities. Merchant and craft guilds formed to protect their members from outside competition and regulate business practices among guild members. By the 1500s, guilds had weakened.

The guild method of production coexisted for a time with the putting-out system, created by merchant-entrepreneurs to supply the growing demand for goods. Putting-out produced a variety of wares for local markets, while wool cloth was the major international trade commodity. Factories making cotton cloth ultimately dislodged putting-out.

2 Looking Back: The Industrial Revolution

No political revolution has touched so many lives as the Industrial Revolution. Africa, Asia, South America—areas of the globe that were not swept by the wave of nineteenth-century industrialization—nevertheless felt its effects. The industrialized countries, determined to acquire colonies, trading ports, and political influence, used their overwhelming military power to gain them. The former colonial areas are now trying to catch up.

The reasons involve national power and standards of living. First, as industrialization proceeds, the labor force shifts from agriculture to manufacturing and service industries.[1] In Western Europe and the United States, agricultural productivity vastly improved during the 1800s. A growing share of the labor force, no longer needed on farms, was drawn to urban industries. The industrialized nations gradually provided more material comforts and longer lives to average citizens.

The infant mortality rate (annual number of deaths of children under age 1 per 1,000 live births) is under 8 in North America, Western Europe, and Japan. The rate is from three to six times higher in developing nations such as Turkey, mainland China, Thailand, and Mexico, and ten times higher in the least-developed countries, such as Nigeria, Uganda, Bangladesh, and Colombia, for example (*Statistical Abstract*, 1994, pp. 854–55).

---

[1]The service (or tertiary) industries include government, education, health care, communications, wholesale and retail trade, insurance, utilities (phones, electricity, gas), and so on; manufacturing and construction are secondary industries. Primary industry refers to agriculture, fishing, mining, and lumbering.

Per capita gross national product (GNP) provides a measure of the relative wealth of nations.[2] According to the *World Development Report* (1993, pp. 238–39), in the low- and lower-middle-income economies of India, Egypt, China, and the Philippines, for example, annual per capita GNP ranged from $80 to $2,500; in the middle-income economies of Mexico, South Korea, Portugal, and Greece, per capita GNP reached nearly $7,000. In the high-income nations the comparable figure was an average of $21,000; with $23,000, the United States was just above the average, and with $34,000, Switzerland was at the peak. A much larger share of the people in nations at the high end of these scales have access to the products and services that can make life pleasant, but most of the world's inhabitants are closer to the lower end. Governments that hope to raise living standards necessarily look to industrial development.

The scientific-technical expertise and factories that accompany industrialization can also provide the know-how and equipment to produce weaponry. In the world as it is, there is no guarantee of national independence. While the United States and the former Soviet Union no longer wage a cold war, the restraints imposed on the foreign policies of their "client states" have also disappeared. Regional threats may shape a suspicious outlook on neighboring countries' intentions, and skepticism about peace-maintaining interventions by other nations or international bodies is easily justified. Industrialization is thus the path to the twin results of better material conditions and modern armaments.

INDUSTRIALIZATION IN ENGLAND

Industrialization involved a shift in production from households to factories, the division of work tasks, the replacement of muscle and wind and waterpower with other sources of energy, and the application of this energy to drive machines (Berg, 1979). Humble cotton cloth, an unlikely candidate for such a historic role, led the way toward industrialization (Ashton, 1969). Stubborn problems had to be faced, but solutions were found.

Industrial Developments

The stumbling block in textile production was a chronic shortage of yarn, which held back the output of weavers. Traditionally, four spinners

---

[2]In the United States, gross national product (GNP) is the annual value of the goods and services attributable to Americans' labor and property in the country and abroad; foreign labor or property in the United States is excluded. Gross domestic product (GDP), the official measure of the U.S. economy adopted in 1991, is the annual value of the goods and services produced by all labor and property located in this country. International comparisons increasingly use GDP, but it is not available for all countries. The differences between GNP and GDP are usually small.

were needed to supply yarn for one weaver. This ratio was upset when John Kay introduced the flying shuttle in 1733. So greatly did this device increase the speed of weaving that either more spinners had to be employed or a method had to be found to spin faster. In the 1760s James Hargreaves invented the spinning jenny, which permitted a worker to spin six or seven threads (eventually 80) all at once. The jenny was small, cheap, and required no great strength to operate. It fit into the domestic system of production but had a serious drawback. Yarn from the jenny was soft and thus suitable only for weft (horizontal strands); the warp (vertical strands) still had to be spun on the slow handwheel. This limitation was overcome by Richard Arkwright, a wigmaker who in 1769 was granted a patent for a frame which produced a yarn strong enough to be used as warp and cheaper than the linen which had often been used. For the first time, a durable and inexpensive all-cotton cloth was made in England. Calico (cloth made entirely of cotton) had previously been imported from India, but shipping costs had boosted its price. Demand for inexpensive English calicoes was immense.

The power needed to drive Arkwright's frame was more than human muscle could deliver, so from the beginning the process was carried out in a factory. Using waterpower, Arkwright set up a factory in 1771 that soon employed some 600 workers, mostly children. Now the old method of carding cotton by hand proved too slow to supply the spinners' needs. To get around this problem, Arkwright devised a way to card mechanically with cylinders. This also required waterpower, so carding and spinning were ordinarily carried out at the same location. Other entrepreneurs quickly established more factories using the new methods of production.

Muslin, a fine cotton cloth, had been imported as a luxury from the Near East. Samuel Crompton, a weaver by trade, built the mule, a water-driven machine that produced both warp and weft for soft yet strong muslin. No longer a luxury, muslins, too, became affordable and extremely popular. After 1790, steam engines powered the mules and other machinery.

The clergyman-poet Edmund Cartwright built a power loom that could be driven by horses, waterwheels, or steam engines. Cartwright's loom proved superior to the frame and mule. By 1815, 30 years after his invention, around 2,400 power looms were in operation; 15 years later, steam was driving 100,000 of them. Handloom weavers made a futile attempt to compete with the factory and steam power. Especially in the woolen and worsted (wool cloth with a smooth, hard surface) branches of the textile industry, hand looms continued to operate into the mid-1800s. Whether woven by hand or mechanically, woolen cloth was more costly than calicoes or muslins and therefore far less in demand at home and abroad.

The printing of calico had been done by craftsmen who used wooden blocks to print the pattern by hand. This changed in the early 1780s when revolving, power-operated cylinders were devised to do the printing. About the same time, new bleaching and dyeing methods, too, were adopted. These processes drew on the discoveries of Scottish and French scientists and were closely tied to the rise of industrial chemistry in England.

By the beginning of the 1800s, manufacturers had integrated all the steps in production and were using steam-driven equipment. The machines built for factories had to be sturdier, due to vibrations, and more durable, because of cost, than was possible with equipment made of wood. Iron was required. Stimulated initially by demand for military gear, the iron industry surged during the eighteenth century. Charcoal, a wood product, was required in smelting iron, but England's forests had been depleted by the seventeenth century, and the price of charcoal had risen. Coal was more plentiful. Experimenters found that when coal is heated, its gases can be removed, leaving a substance called coke that burns with an intense heat and little smoke. In 1783 Henry Cort successfully applied coke to iron making. He heated pig iron (impure iron from the blast furnace) with coke till it became pasty, stirred it until the impurities had burned away, and then passed it between rollers to press out the remaining dross.

Cort's process liberated iron making from dependence on forests and freed England from the need to import iron. Large establishments controlled all the processes, from coal mining to shaping iron objects. Iron, available in unlimited supply, replaced wood in machinery, buildings, and ships.

Cort's inventions, like many others of his time, would have had only a limited effect without a new source of power. Inspired by Theodore Newcomen's "atmospheric engine," James Watt invented the steam engine. Conceived in 1712, the atmospheric engine had been used only for pumping water. A counterweight lifted a piston, then steam under very low pressure flowed into the piston cylinder. When the steam condensed it formed a vacuum, and atmospheric pressure pushed the piston down. While repairing a Newcomen engine in 1765, Watt saw a way to improve its efficiency. To keep the steam in the piston cylinder hot enough to prevent premature condensation, a cylinder jacket and a separate condensation chamber were used. Steam pressure pushing against the piston now did the work. Later, Watt developed a double-acting engine which applied the force of expanding steam to both sides of the piston. If this were not enough, he designed the gears to transmit the engine's action to machinery, and in 1788 he designed a "governor" to automatically maintain the engine's constant speed.

These and numerous other innovations spurred industry, which in turn prompted further inventiveness. The acceleration of patents reflected the tempo of innovation. Before 1760, almost never were more than a dozen patents granted in any single year. In 1761 over 30 were granted; the peak was reached in 1825 with 250 (Ashton, 1969). This outpouring of technical innovations was accompanied by changes in transportation and communication.

Innovations in Transportation and Communication

The movement of people and goods on land had been difficult at best. Roads, with deep mud in winter and clouds of dust in summer, resembled obstacle courses. The main reason was that the communities through which the roads passed were responsible for their upkeep. This changed after 1750 with the formation of turnpike companies, which charged tolls for travel on their roads. On solid foundations, road surfaces were pressed to form a hard finish. As roads became more usable, wagons replaced pack horses and coaches sped passengers to their destinations at 12 miles an hour.

The period from 1760 to 1830 was the canal age. Waterways were dug for barge traffic, knitting England together as never before. Coal, iron, stone, and other bulky commodities were transported more efficiently and much less expensively than earlier. Agricultural products from remote regions reached urban markets, blunting the age-old problem of scarcity in one area and abundance in another. Canal building was nearly a mania; armies of diggers were set to work. To raise the gigantic funds required for these projects, the entrepreneurs who organized canal construction sold transferable shares. As it turned out, the investments were sound.

The utility of canals can be seen in the load that a horse can move: A horse can carry about one-eighth of a ton, pull a one-ton wagon, or draw a barge of 50 tons. Canals thus provided a reliable and relatively cheap means to transport goods.

The most outstanding innovation in transport was the steam locomotive. Inspired by this awesome invention, great cathedral-like terminals were erected to house the engines. As early as 1803, a high-pressure steam engine had been built and run through London's streets. No rails were used because it was believed that a smooth wheel could not get traction on a smooth rail. A dozen years later, it was confirmed in a coal mine that rails and smooth wheels were practical. This led to a much more ambitious project—a 31-mile railroad connecting Liverpool and Manchester. The physical obstacles were formidable: a steep climb at the Liverpool end, bridges to cross, a treacherous marsh. In 1829 the Liverpool and Manchester Railway was completed and the Rocket successfully traveled its tracks (Robbins, 1965).

Once the steam-powered locomotive had been convincingly demonstrated, stronger engines and more railroads soon appeared. By 1850, 6,000 miles of track had been laid; within 20 years this mileage had more than doubled. Although the railroads were built mainly for the movement of freight, by the 1850s passenger traffic provided half of the earnings of railroad companies. Other means of travel could not match the comfort and speed of trains. With three and sometimes four classes of seats, the trains offered people from all walks of life new opportunities for travel. The Great Exhibition of 1851, which celebrated the industrial supremacy of Britain, attracted over 6 million visitors to London, many of whom arrived by train.

In addition to people and freight, trains also carried newspapers and mail. Though it would have been astonishing only 20 years earlier, by the time of the Great Exhibition most areas of the country could receive London's morning newspapers before evening. Within a decade of the Rocket's success, the postal service adopted a device for receiving and distributing mailbags from moving trains. If even greater speed were needed to communicate a brief message, by the mid-1800s people could go to the nearest railway station and make use of Samuel Morse's invention, the telegraph. Before the century ended, another American creation was enthusiastically imported. Alexander Graham Bell's telephone provided instantaneous communication with unexcelled convenience. A young Englishman, Michael Faraday, had constructed a crude generator for producing direct electric current in 1831. A compact generator to produce alternating current was soon built, making possible such devices as the telegraph and telephone.

Social Effects of Industrialization

The technical triumphs of the Industrial Revolution harnessed new sources of energy to drive machines, and physical distance was overcome by inventions which moved people, goods, and messages at undreamed-of speeds. The expanding economy of the 1800s, moreover, offered more opportunities for mobility up the social class ladder than ever before.

All manner of people were drawn into moneymaking activities. Those without resources must work. In England, however, since only the eldest son could inherit his father's title and land, even noblemen's younger sons were obliged to find work. And they did, in medicine, law, politics, teaching, and business. But it was not only that English society was so oddly organized that even the elite's sons sought to make a living; an emphasis on work as a virtuous use of time had crystallized in the secular culture.

The origins of this concept can be traced to the late Middle Ages, especially in Martin Luther's and John Calvin's convictions that work is a form of serving God. (Remnants can be seen in the German word *Beruf*, which combines profession and religious calling.) Several Protestant groups, most notably the Calvinists, had underscored the theme that to waste time in idleness is sinful; time should be used productively. In this theology, religious objections to vigorous participation in the secular world of business were discarded. The Protestant ethic, as it came to be called, developed from these medieval origins (Weber, 1958/1904; Furnham, 1990). But there were obstacles along the way. The moral value of work was usually less apparent to those who could avoid it. If fate generously provided aristocratic or merely wealthy parents, one's time could be spent in more pleasant activities than work.

In the 1700s, the religious impulse to work—perhaps tinged with acquisitiveness—was exercised mainly by the middle classes. The gentleman with land and a title, on the other hand, gladly idled away his days in the manner of this vivid description:

> ...he spent his time as such men have probably spent it from the beginning of things: hunting, shooting, fishing, quarrelling, dicing...; retailing his day's adventures before the fire of an evening, or towsing Liselotte in the barn; riding out on a non-hunting morning to look at his fields, or to call on a neighbor..., and killing the day with a dinner lasting three or four hours. (Lewis, 1957, p. 157)

What was acceptable in the boisterous 1700s, however, was condemned in the mid-1800s. In Queen Victoria's Britain, every stratum of society was encouraged to use time properly:

> ...all respectable early Victorian citizens were expected to fill six days a week with work...; the merely amusing or relaxing, the utterly uneducational, was deprecated as morally feeble.... [For men of all stations] leisure should be devoted to self-improvement, not self-indulgence. (Best, 1972, p. 211)

Although the early religious message that work serves God was still heard from many Protestant pulpits, it was now the worldly desire for respectability that urged work. Religion and secular culture had blended around the theme that steady effort at one's work was a good thing. Of course, all Victorians did not eagerly embrace work, but propriety demanded at least the appearance of well-spent time.

Several other developments were definitely more grim. Industrialization was so rapid that cities could not decently house the workers

over crowding

crowding into them. About 300,000 persons lived in Manchester, Leeds, Birmingham, and Sheffield in 1760; within a hundred years each had grown tenfold to over 300,000 (Hall and Albion, 1953). Cellars and garrets were crammed with families who had little if any privacy for dressing, sleeping, or just relaxing. With the exception of grand houses, the outside privy serving a house or, more likely, several houses was the rule. Excrement dropped into a pit or pail that was emptied sporadically. The mechanical water closet was officially discouraged because sewage systems were inadequate. Not until the late 1890s did sewage systems catch up. Factories, as well as cooking, heating, and gaslight, depended on coal. Soot settled on everything exposed to the air, and just breathing could lead to respiratory ailments. Urban transportation relied on horses, each of which impolitely deposited some 20 pounds of manure on the streets daily. Cities were extremely smelly, grimy, and unsanitary.

Movement to cities was prompted by the pull of higher wages and the push of deteriorating rural conditions. Factory wages were better than those a tenant farmer or agricultural laborer could earn. Even if rural people could earn extra money through putting-out, their earnings were continually forced down by the lower prices of competitive factory-made goods. Moreover, the enclosure of open fields had removed "commons" land from use by tenant farmers and agricultural laborers to graze cows or pigs and gather firewood. In the early 1800s an act of Parliament had eliminated most of the legal obstacles to enclosures, and landlords took this opportunity to proceed. Large numbers of families left the countryside and migrated to cities.

Factory Work

Once in the cities, everyone searched for work. This resulted in child labor, certainly a shocking practice judged by current standards. Yet prior to the Industrial Revolution, children were sent into mines, performed endless farm chores, and worked long and hard under the domestic system. Life was harsh for most people; the view that youngsters should be spared from contributing to their families' survival was a luxury that only a few could afford.

Technical improvements in spinning and weaving made it possible for youths to do factory work. Children as young as 7 years of age toiled in factories for 12 and sometimes 16 hours a day, six days a week, with 40 minutes or so for the day's meal (Thompson, 1964). The owner usually left it to an overseer to administer the factory and to foremen to supervise the work. A foreman with a brutal nature was free to exercise it, and the young workers suffered the most. The foreman was primarily interested in maintaining production, since his wages were linked to output. Especially toward the end of a day, when the children were utterly exhausted, the foreman might strike young workers with a stick to keep them awake for their work and prevent accidents with the machinery.

Legislation began to chip away at child labor in the 1840s. Employers had an obvious interest in hiring youngsters at low wages, and many parents, prompted by necessity or greed, were eager to put their children to work at the earliest possible age. In what remained of cottage industry, the very worst conditions went untouched for a long time. In making hosiery, lace, ribbons, or plaited straw, 5- or even 4-year-old children labored full-time (Best, 1972). By 1870 Parliament had extended the 10-hour day to all workers in officially inspected workplaces, although this still neglected domestic industry. In that same year, however, Parliament accepted and soon enforced the principle that every child under the age of 10 must be a full-time student. With that act the cruel exploitation of young children finally ended.

The conscience of Britain had been aroused by child labor. But it is doubtful that conscience alone would have been sufficient to end the practice. Along with rising industrial output, wages had increased, especially in the last decades of the 1800s (Smelser, 1959). This lessened the hardship of losing a child's income and weakened parents' insistence that their children work. Parliament was dominated by men who had little need to send their young offspring to work, and after a series of investigations reported the terrible conditions of child labor, they were willing to eliminate it.

Conditions of adult work also were generally bitter. Long hours, injury, or even death were confronted by many workers. In most years of the nineteenth century, a thousand English miners were killed and nearly 800 railroad workers died from accidents; in manufacturing, moving parts of machinery, chemicals, and gases added to injury and disease (Best, 1972). The division of labor imposed an exceptionally strict discipline. The tremendous increase in industrial productivity was accompanied by an extreme elaboration of task specialization. Agricultural labor and domestic work can also be grindingly repetitive and dull. There is, nevertheless, the possibility of pauses, slowing down or speeding up one's work at self-determined intervals. It is foolish to romanticize either farm work or cottage industry, yet they did permit a small measure of independence. This vanished in the workplaces in which tasks were subdivided in order to assure the swiftest motions for every operation.

Adam Smith's famous statement on narrowly divided work describes pin making in 1776, just as the Industrial Revolution was gaining momentum:

...a workman not educated to this business... could scarce, perhaps, with his utmost industry, make one pin in a day, and certainly could not make twenty. But in the way in which this business is now carried on, not only the whole work is a peculiar trade, but it is divided into a number of branches, of which the greater part are likewise peculiar trades. One man draws out the wire, another straights it, a third cuts it, a fourth points it, a fifth grinds it at the top for receiving the head; and to make the head required two or three distinct operations; to put it on is a peculiar business, to whiten the pins is another; it is even a trade by itself to put them into the paper; and the important business of making a pin is, in this manner, divided into about eighteen distinct operations, which in some manufactories, are all performed by distinct hands, though in others the same man will sometimes perform two or three of them.

Smith went on to explain why the division of labor was useful:

I have seen a small manufactory of this kind where ten men only were employed, and where some of them consequently performed two or three distinct operations. But...they could, when they exerted themselves, make among them about twelve pounds of pins in a day.... Those ten persons, therefore, could make among them upwards of forty-eight thousand pins in a day.... But if they had all wrought separately and independently, they could certainly not each of them have made twenty.... In every other art and manufacture, the effects of the division of labor are similar to what they are in this very trifling one.... The division of labor, however, so far as it can be introduced, occasions, in every art, a proportionable increase of the productive powers of labor. (Smith, 1937/1776, pp. 4–5)

The more intensive the division of work, the higher the productivity. Many employers attempted to follow this route to maximum output. The disadvantages, however, fell upon the workers who repeated identical movements all day every day. For a large proportion, though certainly not all of them, such routine was then and still is highly monotonous.[3]

Social Class and Reform

The massive social and economic transformations of the Industrial Revolution brought both benefits and ills. Perceiving in industrialization an inherent trend toward increasing misfortune and upheaval, Karl Marx (1867) predicted rising unemployment, declining wages, and the eventual division of the population into two armed camps—the owners of the means of production and the workers who sold their labor. Marx envisioned that through the revolutionary overthrow of capitalism, the exploitation of

---

[3]The techniques of job rotation, enlargement, and enrichment have been proposed to reduce monotony, resulting in scattered though well-publicized applications (Hall, 1994, pp. 287–91; Tausky and Parke, 1976).

labor would end and a politically and economically egalitarian society would ultimately emerge. Although the actual course of events escaped these dramatic predictions, other equally far-reaching changes unfolded.

As a result of the occupations stimulated by the Industrial Revolution, the middle layers of society thickened. A reconstruction of British census data for 1851 and 1881 shows expansion over these years in the professions, particularly teachers, writers, scientists, and lawyers. In commerce, there were increases in clerks, accountants, bankers, and wholesale and retail dealers, and, foreshadowing later developments, more workers were occupied in public administration (Best, 1972).

Expansion of the middle classes led in turn to a spectacular rise in the employment of servants. Their number nearly doubled between 1851 and 1881, and they represented the largest female occupation. When both men and women are included, nearly one out of five of England's entire workforce in the 1880s was in domestic service (Best, 1972). Every family that laid claim to membership in the middle class hired at least a cleaning woman; to display higher status required, minimally, three servants to clean, cook, and serve guests. The wages of servants were low but crept upward as pay generally rose.

Social reform and incomes were helped along by labor organizations. The Combination Act of 1799 had prohibited any association of British workers for the purpose of striking or in any other way combining to influence conditions of work. Trade unions nevertheless were formed and became quietly active among wool combers, hatters, shoemakers, shipwrights, and tailors (Thompson, 1964). Although it was illegal, wages and hours demands were presented to employers. With some they met with success, but other employers brought legal action against the petitioners. The Combination Act was repealed in 1824, largely on the grounds that noninterference was the wisest policy: If workers and employers were left alone to reach their own bargains, unionists would soon realize that combination brought no advantage. However, advantage for the workers there often was. Close on the heels of repeal, a great surge of union joining occurred among miners, building-trades workers, wool combers, and cotton spinners (Thompson, 1964). On occasion, using the now-legal strike, organized workers successfully prodded employers to improve wages and hours.

It remained for a later age to initiate programs for transferring money to those in need. The groundwork was laid by the wealth that industrialization generated and the extension of the vote to working men in 1867. In the first decade of the 1900s, Parliament passed a number of assistance plans. The Workmen's Compensation Act made employers liable for industrial injuries and occupational diseases; the elderly received assistance through a national pension system; and the fear of job loss was eased by unemployment insurance. Before the Industrial Revolution, to seriously propose reducing hardships among a whole population would have seemed insane.

INDUSTRIALIZATION IN THE UNITED STATES

Only the most optimistic observer of the colonial population in America could have believed that it would be the foundation for a nation whose industry would lead the world. In addition to "conventional" immigrants—adventurers, traders, artisans, laborers, farmers—the population was expanded by large numbers of indentured servants, "transported" criminals, and slaves.

Traveling through the towns of Germany, England, and Ireland, hucksters distributed leaflets advertising the abundant wealth of America. Recruiters paid by merchants specializing in importing indentured servants peddled voyages with a fee of seven years of domestic service. Undersupplied with food and overfilled with passengers, the immigrant ships often had mortality rates approaching 50 percent. Criminals were another source of labor in the worker-short economy. English courts could sentence murderers or other criminals to an overseas colony. This relieved England of thousands of undesirable persons and served as punishment, on the presumption that life outside England was worse than imprisonment. Transporting lawbreakers was a profitable business, though not as lucrative as the slave trade.

English, Dutch, and Portuguese ship captains obtained slaves by kidnapping them or by selling rum to African tribal chiefs in exchange for them. Shipboard conditions were especially nightmarish. Regardless, clever arguments in defense of slavery and the slave trade were constructed. This was not surprising, since reputable colonial merchants such as the Cabots and Faneuils were in the slave business, and seaport towns, notably Boston, Salem, New York, and Newport, earned large profits from it. In the 1700s the colonies received about 30,000 slaves a year; by 1800 over half a million slaves had been brought to, or born in, America, accounting for roughly one-quarter of the entire labor force. As late as 1860, the slave proportion of workers was about one-fifth (U.S. Bureau of the Census, 1975, p. 139). Most slaves were sold to plantation owners in the South, since gang labor was impractical on the smaller holdings in the North.

Industry, Commerce, and Agriculture

Industry and commerce developed slowly in the colonies. Furniture, wheels, farm equipment, cloth, and leather, mostly made in homes, were sold in local markets. Furs, fish, and timber were exported, along with Southern tobacco and rice, and, later, the cotton that fed British industrialization.[4] Shipbuilding and the processing of naval stores—pitch, tar, resin, hemp—became significant early industries. Luckily, iron ore was plentiful, and furnaces quickly spread through the colonies (Seligman, 1971).

As in England, American manufacturing was spurred by textiles. An Englishman, posing as a farmer to evade emigration restrictions on mechanics, had memorized the design of Arkwright's yarn-spinning frame. A factory with 72 Arkwright-type frames was opened in 1790 at Pawtucket, Rhode Island, using waterpower to drive the machines. More factories then began to dot the landscape, such as John Lowell's large textile plant in Massachusetts. Housing them in dormitories, he recruited mainly farmers' daughters who were eager to leave the isolated dullness of rural life and earn some money. Company towns with houses, banks, and stores soon appeared; among the thriving towns were Lowell and Lawrence in Massachusetts. The workers' pay was mostly returned to the factory owners through purchases at company stores.

The rubber industry developed from Charles Goodyear's discovery of vulcanizing when he accidentally dropped rubber, sulfur, and lead on a hot stove. A large market for rubber boots launched this industry. By 1850, firearms, clocks, locks, sewing machines, farm equipment, and power-driven machine tools—boring and grinding lathes and a turret lathe with six to eight cutting tools—were being produced in large numbers. The *American system*, as it came to be called, signified the use of standardized, interchangeable parts. Precision lathes made identical pieces that could be interchanged, offering an obvious advantage for mass production and machine repair. Into the 1860s, however, half the nation's factories were still powered by waterwheels, and overall, cottage industry was still dominant.

The outbreak of the Civil War in 1861 delivered a powerful stimulus to American industry—only factories could meet the insatiable demand for military equipment. Factories were built, and steam engines drove the machinery. Within the next few decades, the waterwheel all but disappeared, and a surge of immigration enlarged the work force. By the mid-1890s the value of products manufactured in the United States equaled the combined output of England, France, and Germany (Gutman, 1977). The momentum of industrialization can be seen in the shifting labor force. At the start of the Civil War, the majority of workers

---

[4]Eli Whitney's cotton gin, invented in 1793, cleaned cotton 10 times faster than a person could and helped make cotton a pillar of the South's economy.

were in agriculture; within 30 years, manufacturing accounted for over 60 percent (U.S. Bureau of the Census, 1975, p. 127).

This remarkable expansion of industry was possible because of earlier changes in transportation, agriculture, and the scale of industry. The movement of goods was a difficulty for which a partial solution was found in canals. From small beginnings in New York just before the end of the eighteenth century, the canal system grew to over 3,000 miles by the 1840s, financed with a mix of private and state and local government funds. The canals were so impressive that the crude railroads just coming into use were sneered at as being fit only to provide feeder lines for the canals.

The rickety trains that served most of the states in 1840 were soon improved, however, and railroads became indispensable for transporting people and goods. This accelerated the construction, iron, and coal industries. The extent of enterprise related to trains was immense, accounting for around 15 percent of all capital investment in the 1850s (Seligman, 1971).

Agricultural productivity climbed throughout the nineteenth century. In 1800, for instance, to produce 100 bushels of corn required 340 hours of labor; this fell to about 150 hours by the end of the century (Kranzberg and Gies, 1975). Among mechanical devices, Cyrus McCormick's reaper and John Deere's steel plow were major advances. They were especially useful in the Midwest with its large fields of wheat and corn and heavy soil. Before the end of the century, the reaper had evolved into the agricultural combine, which cut, bundled, and tied grain as it rolled along. Synthetic fertilizer and pesticides and, early in the twentieth century, new varieties of corn and wheat helped boost crop yields. Contributing to the creation and spread of these science-based innovations were the land-grant colleges with their agricultural research and extension services.

The scale of farming also changed, though slowly at first. Interest in large-scale farming had long been present, being most successful in the South where slaves and tenant farmers were available as cheap labor. Farm owners in the Midwest had to compete for labor with the frontier's promise of cheap land and the attractions of urban industry. Nevertheless, the larger-than-family farms survived by using machinery and the help of harvest crews recruited in urban areas. After World War II, large-scale farming and ranching in a corporate form were assisted by the federal government.

The corporate farm is capital-intensive, substituting machinery for labor whenever possible. In the late 1950s the U.S. Internal Revenue Code made shares in corporate farms an appealing investment. The profits of agricultural corporations are allowed to "pass through," meaning that the corporation does not pay federal tax, only its shareholders do. So someone who knows little or nothing about agriculture might nonetheless find farming a good investment. Corporate farms are organized mainly around poultry and eggs, fruit orchards, beef cattle, grain, sugar cane, and vegetables for canning or processing. Corporate farming is thus focused on those products that particularly benefit from large infusions of capital.

Over the years, the number of farms has steadily dwindled. In 1930 there were well over 6 million farms; in 1950, 5 million; and in 1990, just over 2 million (Peterson, 1986; *Statistical Abstract*, 1994, p. 667). About 3 percent of the farms in 1990 were incorporated, some of these actually being incorporated family farms or ranches, but most (the data make no distinction) of them much larger than family members could finance. The 3 percent of farms that are corporate ventures account for over one-third of the value of all farm products sold (*Statistical Abstract*, 1993, p. 653). But whether or not farms take the corporate form, the big ones are the moneymakers. While under 6 percent of all farms have sales of $250,000 or more, they receive over half of all farm sales dollars (*Statistical Abstract*, 1994, p. 670). Not all the larger spreads are corporate ventures, but it is clear that the greatest share of the market for agricultural products is supplied by a relatively few large farms.[5]

Big Business

While a change in tax rules significantly affected agriculture, another federal policy had a much greater economic impact. Although market demands stimulated the rapid climb to world industrial leadership, America's legal framework smoothed the road. Because the U.S. Constitution grants to states the right to charter corporations, each state can design its own laws of incorporation. Eager to attract businesses, many state legislatures made incorporation easy. The matchless advantage of incorporation is the principle of limited liability—the stockholders in a corporation risk only their investments and are not personally liable for the corporation's debts.[6]

Limited liability performed impressively as a vehicle for generating investment, and ease of incorporation further encouraged the growth of business activity (Coleman, 1974). In 1889, New Jersey instituted a

---

[5]With the number of farms declining and income problems among smaller farm operators, rural poverty and unemployment began to rise in the 1970s (Mishel and Bernstein, 1993).

[6]While the shares of joint stock companies could be bought or sold, investors who held such stock were not protected by limited liability. In colonial times, the Plymouth Colony, Jamestown, and New Amsterdam were organized as joint stock companies. By the time England, after much debate, passed the Limited Liabilities Act of 1855, the practice was common in the United States and Western Europe.

variation on laws of incorporation to permit *holding companies,* which own enough stock in other corporations to control their affairs. A number of corporations can thus be formed into a powerful combination. Following the lead of New Jersey, Delaware and Nevada simplified the establishment of holding companies, thus contributing to the shift toward concentration of control. Because of the tactics of men like Andrew Carnegie in steel, John D. Rockefeller in oil, and Cornelius Vanderbilt in railroads, the years following the Civil War became known as "the Age of the Robber Barons."

By a variety of means, business in many sectors of the economy became big business (Seligman, 1971, ch. 3). In 1851 there were 50 telegraph companies; in 1866 Western Union operated 50,000 miles of line and had bought up all except a few remaining telegraph companies. Beginning in 1863 with a modest ironworks, Carnegie expanded into steel production just as the railroads began replacing iron with steel rails; in the 1890s Carnegie's factories controlled two-thirds of steel production in the United States.

Rockefeller invested $5,000 dollars in an oil refinery. The market for kerosene lighting was strong, so he invested in a second refinery, forming the Standard Oil Company of Ohio in 1870. Within the decade, by swallowing rivals through any stratagem, including the most unsavory ones, Standard Oil controlled nearly 90 percent of the nation's refining capacity.

By 1890 the American Tobacco Company had stretched its control over 90 percent of the cigarette business. And meatpacking, too, was consolidated. The giant firms in this industry—Armour, Swift, Cudahy—were formed in the 1880s. From their base in Chicago, the meatpackers shipped endless amounts of meat to the East in refrigerated trains and supplied an increasing number of items retrieved from the bones and hair of cattle and hogs—fertilizers, glue, buttons, combs, felt, glycerine, oleomargarine. The Westinghouse Company, organized initially in 1886 around electricity-generating equipment for public utilities, soon moved into household illumination. Westinghouse was followed in 1892 by General Electric, which soon outmaneuvered and outdistanced it.

The shape of retailing also changed from the small independent store to the consolidated chain. In 1879 Frank Woolworth opened his first successful shop in Lancaster, Pennsylvania, quickly followed by another and another. The key was customer selection of items from open shelves. With his numerous stores Woolworth could buy in quantity and press his suppliers for favorable prices. This, combined with cheap labor— checkout clerks earned $2 to $3 a week—allowed the stores to sell goods at attractive prices. By 1910, a chain of over 70 Woolworth stores had been created. To tap the huge rural market, Aaron Montgomery Ward, in 1871, acted on the idea that a mail order house could supply goods to consumers. About 15 years later, Richard Sears teamed up with A.C. Roebuck to start another mail order business, to which they added a retail outlet, then others, eventually hundreds. In the peak years perhaps as much as $5 of every $100 spent by consumers on merchandise passed through a Sears outlet.

Into the last third of the nineteenth century, business in America was predominantly small business. Then came the great surge of corporate expansion, and the large-scale enterprises of the modern economy appeared (Chandler, 1977). Until 1920, corporate integration best describes the trend: horizontal integration merged firms with similar product lines, and vertical integration extended the scope of firms' activities back into sources of supply and forward to wholesale and retail networks. After 1920, growth through diversification became the rule (Didrichsen, 1977). Buying firms or starting divisions with dissimilar products but similar production processes or distribution channels was the growth strategy of General Electric, General Motors, and DuPont, for instance. Most of the largest manufacturers became highly diversified. A related growth strategy that appeared in the 1950s was the *conglomerate* enterprise, which searches for acquisitions in any venture that offers profitable opportunities.[7] For example, the businesses of one of the largest, the ITT Corporation, include automotive parts, electronic products, Sheraton Hotels, Hartford Insurance, Rayonier forest products, Yellow Pages directories, technical-training institutes, and financial services.

As the scale and complexity of firms grew in the later years of the 1800s, more coordination and oversight of units was needed. Multilayered bureaucracies arose in the attempt to get a firmer grip on operations. The numbers of managers and office personnel swelled with the addition of stenographers, typists, file clerks, bookkeepers, accountants.[8]

Circumstances had overtaken the simple organization in which the owner or his deputy, assisted by a few key men, oversaw the superintendents and checked on the foremen. Through much of the nineteenth century, the control of factory operations was ordinarily in the hands of foremen who hired and fired and set workers' wages. The workers often purchased their own tools, operated machinery at a self-chosen

---

[7]Though now more common, the conglomerate was not a new form of enterprise. In 1790 Alexander Hamilton had helped to organize one of America's earliest conglomerates, which manufactured paper and cotton and linen goods, ran printing shops, and engaged in other activities (Kirsch, 1978, p. xxiv).

[8]Initially, most clerical workers, including typists, were men. (The typewriter was invented in the late 1870s but was neglected for decades.) After the turn of the century, women performed most of the office work (Kanter, 1993).

pace, trained new workers, and coordinated tasks among themselves. In short, the shop floor was largely independent of higher management (Clawson, 1980).

With concern shifting to gaining tighter hierarchical control, new ideas on organization had a chance of being heard. Frederick Taylor's "scientific management" offered a plan that fit the interest in control. Taylor insisted that planning and doing must be separated. It was management's task to design the division of labor, select tools, and determine machine speeds, working pace, rest periods, and the exact motions with which work should be done. After careful studies, management could allocate tasks (preferably small and easily learned) and prescribe time and quality standards for each operation (Taylor, 1947/1911).

At the turn of the century, Taylor had a broad audience for his central theme: Managers should do the thinking, and workers should perform the work.[9] Although workers were considerably less enthusiastic about top-down control, it was popular among managers, and it was effective. The application was pushed furthest with Henry Ford's moving assembly lines—a concept he learned from watching the powered overhead trolleys used for disassembling carcasses in the Chicago meat-packing industry.

When the Model T first appeared in 1908, it cost $850. Refining the assembly process and shifting to a moving production line reduced assembly time to 12 and one-half hours per car and brought down the price. By 1914 assembly time had fallen to 93 minutes. But the speed of work and its repetitive movements created problems in retaining workers. Ford's solution was to offer the stunning $5 day; people lined up at the factory gates for jobs. The Model T was immensely popular. Incredibly, half the cars on the world's roads in the mid-1920s were Fords (Applebaum, 1992).

The basic principles of elaborate division of labor; short, repetitious tasks; and output and time standards urged by Frederick Taylor and so dramatically implemented by Henry Ford became widely accepted as sound managerial techniques for manufacturing, as well as for the processing of papers in large offices. Though Taylor had also advised managers to provide incentive pay to assure workers' motivation to perform in the best way at a brisk pace, this aspect of scientific management was commonly disregarded.

---

[9]In 1918, even the Russian Communist Party Leader Vladimir Lenin praised Taylor's work:
...we must raise the question of applying much of what is scientific and progressive in the Taylor system.... The Taylor system, the last word of capitalism in this respect, like all capitalist progress, is a combination of the refined brutality of bourgeois exploitation and a number of the greatest scientific achievements in the field of analyzing mechanical motions during work.... We must organize in Russia the study and teaching of the Taylor system and systematically try it out and adapt it to our own ends. (Connor, 1968, p. 260)

Workers' Concerns

A day's wage of $5 was a lot of money in 1914. Other employers, shocked by Ford's apparent folly, were fearful of the ideas it might give their workers. Such concerns were premature. Still, incomes were slowly rising, not only in Ford's time but over the last decades of the nineteenth century. Farm hands, laborers, and skilled workers' wages could buy only slightly more in 1880 than at the start of the century. Wages had crept up, but so had prices (U.S. Bureau of the Census, 1975, p. 163; Ware, 1964). Between 1880 and the next two decades, economic expansion brought significant income gains, despite the arrival of 10 million immigrants, many of whom were men seeking work as laborers and factory hands (Yellowitz, 1969). For a five-person family of the 1890s to enjoy some degree of comfort—newspapers, outings, beer, tobacco—required a yearly income of about $500. About half the workers' families were living at that level of income (Montgomery, 1976), but even among them, abundant fortitude was necessary.

Workmen's wives, though usually not in the labor force (except before marriage, and then probably as domestic servants) faced endless chores without the aid of washing machines, gas stoves, or refrigerators. Washing was done by hand, clothes had to be mended, bread baked, and the coal stove which provided heat and cooking demanded frequent attention. Shopping for groceries was a daily task that required ingenuity, since half of the family's income went for food, compared to around 17 percent currently (U.S. Department of Labor, 1979, pp. 22–23; *Statistical Abstract*, 1994, p. 453). Leisure, of course, was a scarcity enjoyed only by the wealthy women with servants.

Working men also needed a good deal of endurance. In 1890, the average workweek in manufacturing was 60 hours; a small unionized segment put in 54 hours. Sunday was the only day off, and paid vacations were a rarity (Ginzberg and Berman, 1964). If a workman was injured on the job, that was his problem. He could sue, but lawyers cost money and employer negligence was difficult to prove. In the late 1920s a few states passed workmen's compensation laws, but in most states the courts were not inclined to interfere with the right of an employer to write labor contracts which placed the risk of injury on the employee.

At the turn of the century, less than 1 percent of the 24 million persons in the labor force were members of trade unions (Ginzberg and Berman, 1964). The American Federation of Labor was organized in the 1880s as an umbrella organization for local craft unions. The potentially large unions in mass-production industries were stifled until federal legislation in the mid-1930s compelled employers to bargain.

By the beginning of the twentieth century, the American economy had created great wealth for a few, modestly comfortable living conditions for many, and quiet desperation among those afflicted by unemployment, poor health, or old age. In the 1930s living standards tumbled as the Great Depression deepened. A quarter of the labor force could not find work; untold others had no alternative but to accept pay cuts and fewer hours. The legislation of the 1930s would be felt most strongly later, when programs such as unemployment insurance and social security were fully implemented.

Before the Great Depression of the 1930s, federal remedies for economic downturns were rejected. Massive long-term unemployment, however, brought the view that government should use fiscal and monetary policies to restrain economic ups and downs. And the rules of economic competition were altered to provide at least minimal protections for the losers. Then as now, controversies over appropriate federal responses to people's economic concerns energize political parties and election campaigns.

SUMMARY

Industrialization first developed in England; by the early 1800s, its factories were the model for producing goods in greater quantities and more cheaply than ever was possible before. Putting-out could not compete with manufacturers' steam-powered machines and their intricate division of labor. With steam applied to transportation, trains moved people and goods swiftly and economically. Canals and paved roads further encouraged commerce between regions.

Enclosures, dwindling incomes from putting-out, and hope of employment in factories drew people to urban areas. When possible, the whole family worked; but often only the women and children were hired for factory work. With cities rapidly growing, newcomers were crowded into cellars and garrets. For all except the grandest homes, sanitation consisted of the outdoor privy, while everyone was exposed to the soot from coal that powered engines, heated homes, provided light, and fueled cooking stoves.

In the early 1800s, British wages were low and conditions of life harsh. Gradually incomes and circumstances improved. Before the century ended, the middle layers of society had expanded, child labor had been nearly eliminated, unions were legal, and working men were allowed to vote. In the early 1900s, employers were made liable for compensation for industrial accidents, and other workers' protection plans were in place. England had become an industrial society in barely over a hundred years.

In the United States, industrialization was quickened by the Civil War's demand for goods. From then on, it advanced so swiftly that by the mid-1890s the value of products made in the United States equaled the combined output of England, France, and Germany. As in England, canals and, especially, railroads sped the growth of industry and commerce.

U.S. agricultural productivity steadily rose in the nineteenth century. The labor force was swollen by workers no longer needed on farms and large numbers of immigrants. Investment in business ventures was encouraged by easy rules for incorporation, since the U.S. Constitution left to the states the right to charter corporate bodies.

In the last decades of the nineteenth century, the contours of the modern American economy became visible, as large, multiunit enterprises were formed. With organizational growth came greater complexity. Coordination and control required an increasing number of managers and office personnel. On the shop floor, workers' tasks were regulated by detailed, top-down plans. Frederick Taylor's concept of scientific management had a lasting influence on the practice of management.

Unions had no legal footing until the mid-1930s, and ordinary citizens' economic positions were unprotected. The Great Depression prodded Congress to pass historic measures that included the right of workers to organize unions and be insured against unemployment.

3 The Labor Force: Making a Living

In 1995, there were about 133 million persons in the U.S. labor force. If the nearly 2 million active members of the armed forces are omitted, the remainder is the *civilian labor force*, the topic discussed here. This labor force has two segments—employed persons and unemployed persons who are available for work.

As defined by the U.S. Department of Labor ("Employment Situation," 1994, p. 5), the labor force includes everyone 16 years of age and older with a particular relationship to work during the *reference week*—the week that includes the 12th day of the month preceding the U.S. Census Bureau's Current Population Survey (CPS), whose primary purpose is to obtain monthly statistics on the labor force. Individuals are counted as *employed* if they:

1. Did any work at all as paid employees during the reference week.
2. Worked in their own business or profession or on their own farm (were self-employed).
3. Worked at least 15 hours without pay in a family business or farm.
4. Were temporarily absent from a job due to illness, bad weather, vacation, strikes, or personal reasons.

Individuals are counted as *unemployed* if they meet all of the following criteria:

1. Had no employment during the reference week.
2. Were available for work during that time.
3. Made specific attempts to find employment (answered advertisements, wrote letters of application) at some time during the four-week period ending with the reference week.

Also classified as unemployed are those who need not be looking for work if they were laid off from jobs and expect to be called back when business picks up. These and other definitions are used in collecting labor force data with surveys of households and businesses, and the Bureau of Labor Statistics releases the data in various publications.

LABOR FORCE PARTICIPATION

The *labor force participation rate* is the percentage of the total population, or of a particular age group, sex, or race, participating in the labor force. Because men have traditionally been expected to work for pay, their participation rates have been fairly stable (see Table 3–1). Women's rates, however, climbed and then soared after 1940, with U.S. intervention in World War II. As the nation swung into expansion of its defense industries, and mobilization of the armed forces, women were needed to replace the men in uniform. A cultural redefinition of women's roles was in the making. Single women, single mothers, divorced women, and, the largest group, wives with low-income-earning husbands, were always most likely to seek paid work. By the 1970s, however, wives with well-paid spouses and those whose mates earned much less were almost equally likely to be in the labor force (Ryscavage, 1979).

TABLE 3–1
Labor Force Participation Rates, United States, 1880–1995

	Total Noninstitutional Population, 16 Years or Older (in millions)	Participation Rate		
		Total	Men	Women
1880	36.8	47%	79%	15%
1900	57.9	50	80	19
1920	82.7	50	78	21
1940	100.1	53	79	25
1960	117.2	59	83	38
1970	137.1	60	80	43
1980	167.7	64	77	52
1990	188.0	66	76	58
1995	197.4	67	75	59

Sources: U.S. Bureau of the Census, *Historical Statistics of the Unites States: Colonial Times to 1979,* Bicentennial Edition (Washington, DC, 1975), Part 2, pp. 127–28; and *Statistical Abstract of the United States, 1994,* p. 396; U.S. Department of Labor, Bureau of Labor Statistics, *Employment and Earnings, 42* (March 1995), pp. 7, 10.

Children also began to make less difference in whether mothers work. Spitze (1988, p. 44) sums this up:

> Over this century, the profile of the typical female worker has changed dramatically. Before 1940, she was young and single, and was expected to stop working for pay after marriage....Between 1940 and 1960, women with school-age children joined the labor force....Since 1960, younger women and mothers of preschool children have shown the most remarkable gains.

This trend is not unique to the United States. Steinberg and Cook (1988, p. 308) review the evidence:

> Although women have been employed in large numbers in times of war, it was not until after the 1950s that their numbers in most labor markets equaled or exceeded their participation in the wartime economies. Since then, female labor force participation rates have climbed steadily, until today, in most industrialized countries, almost half of all adult women are working. More and more of these working women are married and mothers of school-age children.

In just the 33-year span shown in Table 3–2, the percent of American working women jumped in every category.[1]

OCCUPATIONS

When we meet someone for the first time, the conversation is likely to touch on work. Because occupations signal approximate education level, income, and status, discovering another's occupation allows us to estimate the chances of a relationship. People group occupations into categories that they associate with images about the persons in these categories. One such system of grouping became the basis for official data collection.

The Department of Labor periodically revises its *Dictionary of Occupational Titles*, the most inclusive list of occupational descriptions available anywhere. Starting with the 1977 version (the latest is 1991), it includes over 12,000 occupations. But to track occupational trends requires manageable units. This feat was accomplished by Dr. Alba Edwards of the U.S. Census Bureau, who constructed a classification system of six broad categories, organized on the principle of socioeconomic com-

---

[1]A few other significant items on women's participation: Most employed women (three out of four) work full-time. Black, white, and Hispanic women's participation rates are all within the range of 53 to 58 percent. The rate is largest among college graduates and smallest among high school dropouts, and this pattern holds among Hispanic, black, and white women (*Statistical Abstract*, 1994, p. 397).

Table 3–2
Women's Labor Force Participation Rates, United States, 1960 and 1994

	All Women		
	Single	Married	Other
1960	44%	31%	40%
1994	65	61	47
	Women with Children Under 6 years old		
	Single	Married	Other
1960	NA	19%	41%
1994	52%	62	62
	Women with Children 6 to 17 years old		
	Single	Married	Other
1960	NA	39%	66%
1994	68%	76	78

Notes: In 1960, women 14 years old and over were included in the count; thereafter the age range was 16 years and older. "Other" refers to widowed, divorced, or separated. NA indicates "not available."
Sources: U.S. Bureau of the Census, *Statistical Abstract of the United States: 1994*, p. 402; 1994 (March) data provided by Bureau of Labor Statistics, Office of Employment and Unemployment Statistics.

monalties within categories and differences between them. Edwards pulled together Census Bureau returns from 1870 to 1940 to make information available on long-term trends (Wolfbein, 1971, pp. 43–44). He used the following occupational divisions:

1. Professionals.
2. Proprietors, managers, and officials.
3. Clerks and kindred workers.
4. Skilled workers and foremen.
5. Semiskilled workers.
6. Unskilled workers.

The Census Bureau, with some adjustments to reduce Edwards' six categories to four, used his scheme until 1980. It was then changed to a somewhat different six-category system. In order to compare present with prior occupational information, therefore, the data from one classification system must be converted into the other. This was done for Table 3–3, which uses the earlier four-category method to describe changes in the pattern of occupations from 1900 to 1993.

Table 3–3
Occupational Distribution of the U.S. Labor Force, 1900–1995 (in percent)

Occupational Category	1900	1950	1960	1970	1980	1995
White-collar workers	17%	37%	43%	48%	52%	58%
Professional and technical	4	9	11	14	16	18
Managers and officials	6	9	11	11	11	13
Clerical workers	3	12	15	17	19	15
Sales workers	4	7	6	6	6	12
Blue-collar workers	36	41	37	35	32	25
Foreman and skilled workers	10	14	13	13	13	11
Semiskilled workers	13	20	18	18	14	10
Nonfarm laborers	13	7	6	4	5	4
Service workers	9	11	12	12	13	14
Private household workers	5	3	3	2	1	1
Other service workers	4	8	9	10	12	13
Farm workers	38	11	8	4	3	3
Farmers and farm managers	20	7	4	2	2	1
Farm laborers and foremen	18	4	4	2	1	2

Sources: Data for 1900 and 1950, U.S. Bureau of the Census, *Historical Statistics of the United States, Colonial Times to 1970,* Bicentennial Edition (Washington, DC, 1975), Part 2, p. 139; for 1960, 1970, *Statistical Abstract of the United States: 1973,* p. 230; and for 1980 and 1995, U.S. Department of Labor, Bureau of Labor Statistics, *Employment and Earnings,* June 1980, p. 35, and March 1995, p. 27.

Since the turn of the century, white-collar jobs have continually increased. However, since World War II, the trend has been just the opposite for blue-collar work. More than one-fourth of the entire labor force would be semiskilled workers or laborers if the U.S. economy had the same mix of work today as it did in 1950. The expansion of some white-collar jobs generated better opportunities, but others did not—jobs in professional-technical and managers-officials categories provide more advantages than those in clerical or sales work. The growth of service workers' jobs provides mixed opportunities.

The service workers category includes a diversity of jobs, many at the lowest levels of an occupational cluster. In food services, for instance, waitresses, waiters, dishwashers, and cooks are considered service workers, but bakers are counted as skilled workers, and food-service supervisors are classified as managers. In health services, practical nurses and attendants are included as service workers, while registered nurses are in the professional-technical category. Also among service workers are firefighters, police and detectives, barbers and beauticians, guards, doorkeepers, watchmen, porters, janitors and bootblacks. Many of these are low-skill, minimum-wage occupations. Overall, then, changes in the distribution of occupations indicate favorable openings for people who can take advantage of growth in the high-education, high-skill sectors (professional, managerial, technical jobs), and less favorable consequences for others.

According to the U.S. Department of Labor ("Usual Weekly Earnings," 1994), the relation between educational level and the weekly median income of full-time wage and salary workers follows this pattern:

Less than a high school diploma	$310
High school graduate, no college	424
Some college or associate degree	496
Bachelor's degree	666
Advanced degree	865

The connection between education and income holds among women and men and among racial groups, although the dollar amounts are not identical. Education pays.

Years of schooling have consistently moved up among members of the labor force. In each decade since 1940, a year has been added to the median years of education for workers; it is now about 13 years (*Statistical Abstract*, 1994, p. 158). Employers have raised the level of education required to get a job-candidate's foot in the door, because the time spent at school does not alone guarantee quality of education, and workers with higher levels of schooling are available.

Although most American workers finish high school, not all do. In 1993, about 10 percent of whites, 15 percent of blacks, and almost 40 percent of Hispanics in the labor force had not graduated from high school. On the upper end of the education stairway, white workers are much more likely to be college graduates than are black or Hispanic workers (*Statistical Abstract*, 1994, p. 397). We will discuss college degrees later.

Who Gets Which Jobs?

Focusing on gender and race, Table 3–4 indicates which categories of workers are in which jobs. Highly skilled blue-collar work (precision production, craft, and repair) is almost exclusively done by men, and this is true, too, for driving transportation equipment or working as a helper or laborer. In the executives and managers category, there are heftier proportions of white women and men than of blacks. Studies indicate that in large companies women of any color seldom reach the top layers (assistant vice-president or above). The proportion of women holding such positions in the 1990s climbed to around 7 percent in the nation's 1,000 largest companies, but this is from a very small base of under 3 percent in the late 1970s (U.S. Department of Labor, 1991; Kanter, 1993). In contrast, over one-third of all working women are found in

Table 3–4
Occupations, by Gender and Race, United States, 1995 (in percent)

Occupational Category	Total Labor Force	Men		Women	
		White	Black	White	Black
Managers and professionals	*28%*	*28%*	*17%*	*30%*	*21%*
Executive, managerial	13	15	9	13	9
Professional specialty	15	13	8	17	12
Technical, sales, and administrative support	*30*	*20*	*18*	*43*	*39*
Technical	3	3	3	4	4
Sales	12	12	7	13	10
Administrative support, including clerical	15	5	8	26	25
Service occupations	*14*	*9*	*18*	*17*	*27*
Private household	1	–	–	1	2
Protective service	2	3	5	1	2
Other services	11	6	13	15	23
Precision production, craft, and repair	*11*	*19*	*13*	*2*	*2*
Operators, fabricators, and laborers	*14*	*20*	*32*	*7*	*11*
Machine operators, assemblers, and inspectors	6	7	11	5	8
Transportation and material moving occupations	4	7	11	1	1
Handlers, equipment cleaners, helpers, and laborers	4	6	10	1	2
Farming, forestry and fishing	*3*	*4*	*2*	*1*	–

Note: Total labor force includes Hispanic and Asian workers. A dash (–) indicates less than half of 1 percent of workers.

Source: U.S. Department of Labor, Bureau of Labor Statistics, *Employment and Earnings, 42* (March 1995), p. 28.

"administrative support, including clerical" or sales. A sizable fraction of women also are employed in "other services" (the "other service workers" in Table 3–3), and which include nurses aides and orderlies, food servers, and child care providers.

About 8 percent of workers are Hispanic, 10 percent are black, and 2 percent are Asian; the remainder are white males (44 percent) or white females (36 percent) (*Statistical Abstract*, 1993, pp. 401, 405; "White, Male, and Worried," 1994, pp. 52–53). The occupational patterns of Hispanic workers (not shown in Table 3–4), indicate that Hispanic men are most often employed as service workers or in other low-skilled jobs (operators, fabricators, laborers). The occupations of Hispanic women are also highly concentrated; well over half are in sales, administrative support, or the service occupations. On a brighter note, one out of five Hispanic men is in a highly skilled blue-collar occupation, and nearly the same proportion of Hispanic women are either managers or professionals (Cattan, 1993).

Considering access to jobs over several decades also is revealing. In 1960, only a tiny fraction (4 percent) of black men were managers or professionals, while one out of four were laborers. In that same year, nearly 40 percent of black working women were domestic servants (*Statistical Abstract*, 1983, pp. 386–90). Significant occupational upgrading of black workers is visible between 1960 and the 1990s. White women also experienced occupational gains, though the results are less striking; a larger share in 1960 had been employed as semiskilled factory and service workers or in clerical jobs (U.S. Department of Labor, 1975b). In these 30-plus years, there were modest shifts from these occupations into managerial and professional positions.

Two developments that we might reasonably suppose have helped to ease occupational disparities between the sexes and races are equal employment opportunity and affirmative action regulations, and more similar educational credentials. Government enforcement of equal employment opportunities has had mixed reviews, not only because it creates paperwork for employers but also in terms of results. The weight of the evidence, however, suggests at least some favorable outcomes. Enforcement of equal opportunity provisions has contributed to a measurable degree of occupational upgrading, but mainly among black men and women with college degrees. Put another way, women and minority workers as a whole have not been helped much by government programs—already-advantaged women and minorities are the main beneficiaries. Observers reported this result years ago and continue to do so (Butler and Heckman, 1977; Tomaskovic-Devey, 1993).

Clearly, more women and minorities are earning college degrees, as indicated in Table 3–5. The substantial gap between white males and others is slowly shrinking. The data for Asian women and men show that they are earning college degrees at the highest rate of all categories. The value Asian parents place on education and tight family structures that support college attendance go a long way toward explaining such graduation rates (the proportion of postgraduate degrees earned by Asians is also higher). Overall, a growing portion of all segments of the population are earning college degrees. This contributes to occupational advances, while expanding the competition for desirable jobs.

SERVICE-PRODUCING AND GOODS-PRODUCING INDUSTRIES

Another aspect of occupations is the industries in which they are located. A worker might be a manager, secretary, or repair person in either an insurance company or a manufacturing firm. Both are industries, but

Table 3–5
College Graduates, by Race, Ethnicity, and Sex, United States, 1960–1993

Persons Age 25 and Over	Percent Completing 4 Years of College or More			
	1960	1970	1980	1993
All persons	8%	11%	16%	22%
White				
Men	10	15	22	26
Women	6	9	14	20
Black				
Men	3	5	8	12
Women	3	5	8	12
Hispanic				
Men	NA	8	9	10
Women	NA	4	6	9
Asian				
Men	NA	NA	NA	43
Women	NA	NA	NA	36

Note: Persons of Hispanic origin may be of any race. The data for Asians are for 1991 and include Pacific Islanders.
Source: U.S. Bureau of the Census, Statistical Abstract of the United States: 1994, p. 157.

the insurance company is classified as service-producing and the manufacturing firm as goods-producing.

In industrial societies, as we mentioned earlier, a growing portion of employment is generated by the service sector. Table 3–6 shows that American service industries have indeed expanded and in 1995 accounted for nearly 80 percent of employment. The largest, most consistent rise has been in business, personal, and professional services. In 1890, many of the activities in this cluster would have been done by household servants. This occupation has all but disappeared, while the other services have increased and are still headed up. Government, too, has been a relatively high-growth sector, although it peaked around the 1970s. The expansion was strongest at the state and local levels, which together employ four out of five government workers. With a combined workforce of 16 million, federal, state, and local governments have become major employers. At a slow though steady pace, trade has also expanded; the largest share is retail trade, which accounts for most of the increase.

While the service-producing sector has consistently expanded, the goods-producing sector has declined. Manufacturing entered the 1950s with a husky share of total employment, but manufacturing jobs steadily disappeared as the years passed. There is no mistaking the fact that the

Table 3–6
**Employment in Goods-Producing and Service-Producing Industries,
United States, 1890–1995**

Industry	Percent of Workers Employed				
	1890	1950	1970	1980	1995
Service-producing industries	*29%*	*51%*	*64%*	*71%*	*78%*
Finance, insurance, real estate	1	4	5	6	6
Business, personal, professional services	11	10	16	20	28
Trade: wholesale and retail	8	18	20	22	23
Transportation, utilities, communications	6	8	6	6	5
Government: federal, state, local	3	11	17	17	16
Goods-producing industries	*71*	*49*	*36*	*29*	*22*
Manufacturing	20	29	26	21	15
Construction	6	4	5	4	4
Farming, forestry, mining, fishing	45	16	5	4	3
Total employed labor force (in millions)	23.7	58.9	78.6	99.3	125.6

Note: Business, personal, and professional services include, for example, consulting and legal services, health services, private education, repair, entertainment, hotel and motel services, barber and beauty shops, cleaning, gardening, and private household services.

Sources: 1890 data based on U.S. Bureau of the Census, *Historical Statistics of the U.S., Colonial Times to 1970*, Bicentennial Edition (Washington, DC, 1975), Part 1, pp. 138–39; 1950 data from *Statistical Abstract of the United States: 1974*, p. 228; 1970, 1980, and 1995 data are from U.S. Department of Labor, Bureau of Labor Statistics, *Employment and Earnings, 41* (December 1994), pp. 35, 51, and *42* (March 1995), pp. 29, 44.

massive shift of employment from goods-producing to service-producing industries has been a long-term development. True, growth in services has offset losses in goods production, but there are reasons to regret that so many manufacturing jobs have vanished. Compared to service businesses, manufacturing firms tend to be bigger, their markets are less fragmented, profit margins are somewhat thicker, and there is more union presence. Each of these factors can affect pay. On average, compensation of manufacturing workers (wages plus such benefits as medical insurance) is 20 percent ahead of that for service-producers (Mishel and Bernstein, 1993). With a smaller proportion of manufacturing jobs, the opportunities for good earnings are reduced, especially for workers without college degrees.

Manufacturing, however, has a larger impact on the U.S. economy than the sagging employment figures alone might suggest. American manufacturing firms now directly add just 20 percent to the gross domestic product, but manufacturers also need what other businesses provide—raw materials, construction, janitorial and groundskeeping services, utilities, transportation, consulting, advertising, marketing, accounting and legal services, insurance, banks, stock and bond underwriters, and so forth. These purchases by goods-producing industries greatly amplify their economic impact.

OTHER SECTORS OF THE LABOR FORCE

People who are unemployed but looking for work are part of the labor force. But there are also the underemployed—part-time or temporary workers who would prefer full-time work and those whose jobs do not measure up to their capabilities. Part-timers, temporary workers, and a group called independent contractors are considered part of the growing contingent workforce.

Unemployment

Unemployment may be *seasonal* (some occupations, such as construction or picking crops, require workers for only part of a year), *cyclical* (ups and downs that result from periodic economic fluctuations), or frictional or structural (Bronfenbrenner, Sichel, and Gardner, 1987). *Frictional unemployment* refers to short-term unemployment after quitting or losing a job and before finding another. Economists suggest that due to frictional and seasonal causes, an unemployment rate of around 6 percent is normal, even in good times. Most ominous is *structural unemployment*, the long-term or permanent job losses resulting from technological or market changes that affect an industry. Older workers are especially at risk, since they may find it difficult to learn new skills or to find other employment. The steel, automobile, consumer electronics, textile, and, most recently, a variety of defense industries have been large contributors to American structural unemployment.

Unemployment fluctuates over time, as shown in Table 3–7. The deepest unemployment in the 100–plus years covered in the table was during the Great Depression of the 1930s, but with America's entry into World War II, the rate soon fell to its lowest point, under 2 percent. Such a low rate is unlikely to recur. If the economy expands at a clip that steeply reduces unemployment (say to around 5 percent), the Federal Reserve Board becomes nervous about the potential inflationary consequences of an "overheated" economy. It then acts to slow the economy, and unemployment generally starts to rise. (The operations of the Federal Reserve Board are discussed further in Chapter 5.)

Unemployment also affects workforce segments differently. Table 3–8 indicates the characteristics that contribute most to the unemployment rate: poor education, lack of skills, minority status, and youth. Though the rates vary over time, the relationships persist. Women who maintain

Table 3–7
U.S. Unemployment Rates, 1890–1994

1890	4.0%	1975	8.3%
1895	13.7	1976	7.6
1900	5.0	1977	6.9
1920	5.2	1978	6.0
1929	3.2	1979	5.8
1930	8.7	1980	7.0
1933	24.9	1981	7.5
1940	14.6	1982	9.7
1941	9.9	1983	9.5
1943	1.9	1984	7.4
1944	1.2	1985	7.1
1945	1.9	1986	6.9
1950	5.3	1987	6.1
1960	5.4	1988	5.4
1970	4.8	1989	5.2
1971	5.8	1990	5.4
1972	5.5	1991	6.6
1973	4.8	1992	7.3
1974	5.5	1993	6.7
		1994	5.9

Sources: Data for 1890–1929, U.S. Bureau of the Census, *Historical Statistics of the U.S., Colonial Times to 1979*, Bicentennial Edition (Washington, DC, 1975), Part 1, p. 135; for 1930 to 1950, Philip L. Rones and Carol Leon, *Employment and Earnings During 1978*, Special Labor Force Report no. 218 (Washington, DC: Bureau of Labor Statistics, 1979), p. A-4; for 1950, U.S. Department of Labor, *Manpower Report of the President* (Washington, DC, 1975), p. 203; and for 1960–1994, *Employment and Earnings, 42* (March 1995), p. 9.

families have markedly high unemployment, especially black and Hispanic women. Because education, job skills, and minority status are intertwined, when the economy slumps and unemployment generally rises, the rates for low-skilled minority workers are higher—a rule of thumb suggests twice as high.

International comparisons of unemployment are shown in Table 3–9. Over the years the U.S. unemployment rate has been lower than in some industrialized countries and higher than in others. In the 1990s, however, unemployment has climbed in most of the industrialized nations. (We return to this point later.) In 1995, Japan's unemployment rate inched up to over 3 percent, the highest in 40 years, and Western Europe's reached an average of 11 percent ("Europe's High Taxes," 1995).

Underemployment and the Contingent Workforce

Underemployment refers to workers who have part-time jobs (officially counted as less than 35 hours a week) but who prefer full-time employ-

Table 3–8
Unemployment Rates and Selected Worker Characteristics,
United States, 1995

Characteristics	Percent Unemployed
Race, ethnicity, gender, and age	
White, total	4.7%
Men: 20 years and over	4.0
16 to 19 years	17.7
Women: 20 years and over	4.1
16 to 19 years	13.9
Black, total	10.1
Men: 20 years and over	7.9
16 to 19 years	40.2
Women: 20 years and over	9.0
16 to 19 years	31.3
Hispanic origin, total	9.2
Men: 20 years and over	7.0
16 to 19 years	25.9
Women: 20 years and over	8.8
16 to 19 years	25.0
Education	
Less than high school	13.5
High school graduate	6.4
Some college, no degree	5.5
Associate degree	4.0
Bachelor's degree	2.7
Master's degree	2.3
Professional or doctoral degree	1.6
Family status	
Married men, spouse present	3.0
Married women, spouse present	3.6
Women who maintain families	8.1
Occupation	
Managers	2.3
Professionals	2.5
Technicians	2.8
Sales	5.3
Administrative support, including clerical	4.2
Private household workers	9.8
Protective services	2.9
Other services	8.1
Precision production, craft, and repair	7.0
Operators, fabricators, and laborers	9.3
Farming, forestry, and fishing	10.5
Type of worker	
Full-time	5.3
Part-time	6.0

Table 3–8 continued

Characteristics	Percent Unemployed
Industry	
Goods-producing	5.5
Manufacturing	4.4
Construction	10.5
Agriculture	9.1
Service-producing	4.5
Trade: wholesale and retail	6.4
Finance	3.5
Government	2.8

Note: Education data are for 1994.
Sources: U.S. Department of Labor, Bureau of Labor Statistics, *Employment and Earnings, 42* (March 1995), pp. 12–13, 18, 36. Data on Hispanic unemployment rates, and education and unemployment, provided by the Bureau of Labor Statistics, Office of Employment and Unemployment Statistics.

Table 3–9
Unemployment Rates in Selected Industrialized Countries,
Adjusted to U.S. Concepts, 1960–1995

	1960	1970	1984	1988	1991	1993	1995
United States	5.5	4.9	7.5	5.5	6.7	6.8	5.7
Canada	7.0	5.7	11.2	7.8	10.3	11.2	9.6
Australia	1.6	1.4	9.0	7.2	9.6	10.9	8.3
Japan	1.7	1.2	2.8	2.5	2.1	2.5	3.2
France	1.9	2.6	10.0	10.2	9.6	11.8	12.4
West Germany	.8	.8	7.1	6.3	4.4	6.0	6.5
Italy	NA	5.4	5.9	7.9	6.9	10.3	12.2
Sweden	1.5	1.5	3.1	1.6	2.6	9.3	9.8
United Kingdom	2.2	3.1	11.8	8.6	8.8	10.4	8.6

Sources: Joyanna Moy and Constance Sorrentino, "Unemployment, Labor Force Trends, and Layoff Practices in 10 Countries," *Monthly Labor Review, 104* (December 1981), pp. 4–5; "Employment Change in 10 Countries," *Monthly Labor Review, 116* (October 1993), p. 132. Data for 1993 and 1995 (July) were provided by the Bureau of Labor Statistics, Division of Foreign Labor Statistics.

ment, temporary workers who want stable work, or persons with jobs for which they are overqualified (a teacher working as a teacher's aide, for instance).[2] Underemployment thus means workers are not fully utilized.

The *contingent workforce* includes part-time and temporary workers and independent contractors. Temporary workers may be hired directly

[2]Part-time workers have gradually increased to around 20 percent of the labor force. Two out of three are women, and the majority of part-timers report that they prefer that arrangement (*Statistical Abstract*, 1993, p. 402; "Employment Situation: May 1994").

by a firm or assigned to jobs by a temporary help agency. These agencies match workers with employers, pay the workers, and may offer them benefits (though there are often hurdles to qualifying for them). Independent contractors make their own arrangements directly with an employer who needs an employee. Independent contractors are self-employed and must make their own payments for unemployment insurance, Social Security, and health insurance. Whether assigned by an agency or hired directly as a temp or an independent contractor, such employment is unstable and dependent on employers' short-term needs. The concept of a contingent workforce thus is characterized by loose ties between workers and employers.

Especially in recent years, the use of temporary or contract workers has become more attractive to employers, due to stiffer competition and concerns about fixed costs. Temporary workers and independent contractors can easily be added or shed. They can handle workload fluctuations, meet seasonal demands, undertake special projects, fill in for vacancies and buffer the regular workforce if downturns occur (Carre, 1992). Contingent workers are available for all sorts of assignments, from production to professional and administrative tasks, and they are found in all industries.

Contingent workers offer another advantage: They are frequently less costly than regular workers. Temporary employees—whether hired from an agency or directly—are often ineligible under federal and state laws for unemployment compensation. This insurance is costly to employers, who also do not need to offer temporary workers other benefits their regular workers might have, such as medical insurance and retirement plans. Independent contractors must individually reach agreements with prospective employers, who may be reluctant to provide such benefits. For the employer, therefore, hiring contingent workers may seem a wise plan, but damaging results have also been observed (Carre, 1992). Temporary workers form no bonds with a company; they have no commitment to its future success. Immediate labor cost savings may handicap long-term productivity gains.

Temporary-help agencies grew rapidly in the 1980s, and they have provided employers with growing numbers of workers in the 1990s ("O.K., Back to Work," 1993). They place about 2.5 million workers annually ("Experimenting with Temps," 1993), and in addition probably a million persons are employed as contract workers at any one time. More important than these numbers is that the contingent-worker segment of the labor force is growing faster than the regular full-time force. A policy of employee staffing for low-demand conditions and adding temporary workers for peaks and special projects is seen as effective by many American companies. Frito-Lay, Johnson and Johnson, Motorola, and Miller Brewing, for instance, have used contingent workers.

WORK OUTCOMES

Work outcomes are the consequences of working, the glue that attaches people to their work. The following list gives some idea of the range of outcomes for workers:

1. Without work, the hours may drag by; work prevents a feeling of drift, aimlessness.
2. Work provides a culturally approved means of obtaining income.
3. Work is a basis for being the head of one's household or a partner in supporting the family.
4. The content of work may be experienced as pleasing.
5. A job's features (prestige, income), or simply holding a job, may raise one's self-esteem.

In this section we examine three major work outcomes—income, prestige, and satisfaction. Before looking at them, however, we need to consider two other features of work. First, most people earn a living by working for others; only about 10 percent of the U.S. labor force is self-employed.[3] Second, small businesses employ a large part of the work-force. Table 3–10 shows the 1980 and 1990 distributions of workers in organizations of various employee-size classes. These data are based on *establishments*, a location for production or a service. The separate locations of multiunit companies are each counted. Most firms, 8 out of 10, have only one site (*Statistical Abstract*, 1993, p. 742).

The first row in Table 3–10, indicates that over 50 percent of the millions of organizations in 1980 and 1990 had no more than four employees. Employee-size classes under 20 include over 85 percent of organizations and about 25 percent of all employees. At the other extreme, in the employee-size class of 1,000 and over, a tiny fraction

---

[3]Self-employment data are collected by government agencies that use different methods (*Statistical Abstract*, 1993, pp. 402, 532). The Current Population Surveys of American households count the *unincorporated* self-employed. A worker who incorporates a business is classified as employed by a firm. The Internal Revenue Service, using tax returns, counts unincorporated sole proprietorships and partnerships. The method of counting thus influences what is included as self-employment. Aronson (1991) examined the available information. Among his conclusions: the majority of self-employed are men; the industries with the largest numbers of self-employed are personal and business services, retail trade, and construction; and the proportions of self-employment in Western Europe are generally similar to those in the United States.

Table 3–10
Employment by Size of Employing Organization, United States, 1980 and 1990

Employee-Size Class	Percent of Employees in Class		Percent of Employing Organizations in Class	
	1980	1990	1980	1990
1–4	6.7%	6.3%	54.3%	54.2%
5–9	8.5	8.7	19.8	20.1
10–19	10.8	11.1	12.4	12.5
20–49	15.9	16.4	8.3	8.1
50–99	12.4	12.9	2.9	2.8
100–249	14.4	15.6	1.6	1.6
250–499	9.4	8.9	.4	.4
500–999	7.6	7.0	.2	.2
1,000 or more	14.3	13.1	.1	.1

Total number of employees
1980: 74.8 million
1990: 93.5 million
Total number of organizations
1980: 4.5 million
1990: 6.2 million

Note: Organizations here represent establishments, a single physical location where a service or production is performed. Companies with establishments in several locations report each separately. Data for employees of establishments exempt from the Social Security Act are excluded.

Sources: U.S. Bureau of the Census, *County Business Patterns 1980: United States,* and *1990: United States* (Washington, DC, 1982 and 1993), Figure 2.

of 1 percent of organizations employ about 13 percent of the workforce.

Overall, then, the chances are about equal that a person will work in an organization with either less than or more than 100 employees. But large corporations are certainly the most economically potent, no doubt about it, and many small companies survive by supplying products or services to large ones, often on the big companies' terms (Harrison, 1994). Ranked by business receipts, the top 2 percent of companies in 1990 garnered nearly 80 percent of total gross corporate income, while companies with receipts under $1 million (this includes over 80 percent of corporations) collected just 6 percent of total revenues (*Statistical Abstract,* 1994, p. 540). One problem with working in a small business is that its resources to cushion economic troubles—cash reserves, access to credit, peripheral plants or equipment that might be sold—are limited. Not surprisingly, small enterprises, especially start-ups, have high failure rates; over half are out of business within six years (Boyett and Conn, 1992).

Income

The question of who receives what from work and why they get it easily draws us into issues of justice. Yet whatever exists can be taken for granted. When over the centuries the world's work was done by slaves, serfs, and peasants, they made do with what the customs of the times provided, and abstract, intellectual curiosity about it was meager. Interest rose, however, with the onset of the Industrial Revolution. Factories multiplied and with them the wage earners whose level of pay was not ordered by custom.

Early Explanations of Income

Most attention to income had concentrated on the source of national wealth. From the 1500s into the 1800s, the prevailing doctrine was *mercantilism*, based on the principle that a nation's wealth is increased in a manner similar to a merchant's. To prosper, the value of the goods a nation sells (exports) must be larger than the cost of the goods it buys (imports). Government's role, therefore, is to expand external markets while protecting the home market.

Tariffs on imports, and colonies to provide raw materials and buy the home country's products, were central policies in the pursuit of national wealth. The economic quarrels inspired by this doctrine were only a short step from political struggles. Commenting on the American experience, Robert Reich (1992, p. 15) notes, "There were, of course, other reasons why the American colonies sought independence from England, but had they been able to develop their own economies uninhibited by England's mercantilist demands, the separation would have occurred much later, and probably more peacefully."

A challenge to the mercantilist doctrine came from members of an early school of political economy in the 1700s. These *Physiocrats* argued that a nation's prosperity is derived from the land and water—the farmer, miner, and fisherman are the only true producers of wealth, and tariffs should be abolished because they raise the prices of manufactured goods. These early advocates of laissez-faire economics urged that government should avoid involvement in economic affairs.

Adam Smith focused his income theory directly on the organization of production. In *The Wealth of Nations* (1937/1776), he proposed a uniquely different understanding of income: Wealth is created by greater productivity, and productivity grows by combining efficient machinery with an intensive division of labor. The more that is produced in relation to population, the better off will the average person be. National wealth and individuals' economic improvement thus depend on industrial efficiency. Smith asserted that wages will not rise in a static economy. The necessary condition for higher wages is a growing economy in which employers compete for workers.

Other theorists expressed a gloomier outlook. David Ricardo (1821) explained that income would always remain close to the subsistence level because the demand for labor and the supply of labor inevitably caused wages to fluctuate around the amount that would maintain a worker and his family at the subsistence level. Higher pay would increase the supply of workers because more children would survive into adulthood; they would swell the labor supply, and wages would sink below the level of subsistence. As a result, fewer children would survive, creating a labor shortage. Employers would then have to compete for workers by raising wages above the level of subsistence, and the cycle would be repeated. Ricardo's "iron law of wages," as this theory came to be called, received wide attention. Before long the basic idea was endorsed by Karl Marx, as the Industrial Revolution swirled around him.

Marx—economist, historian, revolutionary—agreed that wages could not long stay above workers' subsistence needs, though for different reasons than Ricardo's. In *Capital* (1906/1867), Marx reasoned that the operation of a capitalist system suppresses wages. Workers consistently earn less than their employers receive when they sell the final products, so the employers gain profits. Marx called profit "surplus value" and saw it as exploitation of labor. If the employer introduces new machinery to raise the workers' output, wages do not increase accordingly. Since other employers are also attempting to increase profits and remain competitive, they also invest in more efficient machinery. Capitalism therefore tends to produce more goods than the market can absorb. Excess production creates recurring periods of falling wages and rising unemployment, and each recession leaves a larger pool of unemployed. Marx expected the overthrow of capitalism would result as these conditions worsened.

Modern Wage Theories

More-modern wage theories also sharply differ. Four are discussed here. The first—marginal productivity—is important in economics, the second—functional importance and scarcity—in sociology, and the last two—dual labor markets and comparable worth—have an audience in both disciplines.

First, according to the *marginal productivity* (or marginal analysis) theory of income, an employer's decision to hire one more worker is rational if the marginal cost (the cost of hiring one more worker) is less than the marginal benefit (the increased value of the output due to that additional worker). The wage for a particular kind of work will approach the value of the output that is gained by hiring that last worker, and his or her wage will determine the wages of previously hired employees performing similar jobs. In a nutshell, an employer will hire a worker if the economic benefits to the firm are greater than the costs, and wages reflect workers' relative *contributions* to the total value of the output. However, it is doubtful that employers actually know the relative contributions of employees to output. So while marginal productivity theory can usefully be applied to hiring in market economies, it leaves much to be desired as a guide to income decisions.

Second, a major sociological attempt to explain income differences as well as prestige (Davis and Moore, 1945), is based on the assumptions that the world of work contains jobs which differ in both the degree of difficulty of finding qualified workers (*scarcity* of trained personnel) and the consequences to an employer if a position is not filled (*functional importance* of a task). The theory thus concludes that the hierarchical distribution of occupational income and prestige reflects differences in functional importance and scarcity of competent personnel. Moreover, this distribution is motivationally necessary. Individuals would not undertake lengthy training unless the occupations that require such preparation offer greater rewards than less-demanding jobs do. The interpretation of functional importance (a concept similar to contribution in marginal productivity theory) has aroused controversy since it was introduced (Tumin, 1953; Hall, 1994).

Functional importance is best understood as residing in the eye of the beholder. Is the doctor or garbage collector more crucial to public health? Is the engineer or assembly-line worker more central to production? Though the choices are debatable, it is clear that doctors and engineers require more training. The issue shifts, then, from functional importance to what motivates people to undertake training? On this point, Davis and Moore are basically right. To encourage individuals to undergo training, they must expect that it leads to jobs that make the investment in training worthwhile. But now another problem surfaces: Just how much does it take to attract people to one occupation instead of another, or to lead them to accept broader responsibilities? Must the doctor's compensation exceed that of a nurse by 150 percent, or is 50 or 15 percent enough? Must the CEO of a company receive double the income of a division head? For these questions, the original theory is of little help. It proposes, essentially, that people accept what they can get.

Alternatively, some perspectives view people as getting what they can take. Suggestions along these lines have come from Marxist, conflict, exchange, and sociobiology theories. Recall that according to Marx, factory owners keep as much of the profits as possible while passing on to labor as little as possible. Similarly, Collins (1975, pp. 60–61), an advocate of conflict theory, noted that "each individual is basically pursuing his own interests and…there are many situations, notably ones where power is involved, in which those interests are inherently antagonistic.… Social structures are to be explained in terms of the behavior following from various lineups of resources." And when sociobiology explains humans' actions, as van den Berghe (1991, p. 272) observes, "It regards behavior as either self-serving or misguided; it explains away apparent altruism as sophisticated selfishness…; it presents, in short, a thoroughly cynical view of human action." The emphasis here is on self-interest, a plausible assertion when economic gain or loss is at stake.

The third approach is *dual labor markets* (Hodson and Kaufman, 1982; Hodson and Sullivan, 1995). The labor force is viewed as employed in two economic sectors—a core and a secondary (or peripheral) sector. The core sector is *oligopolistic* industries in which a few big companies have a large share of a market (for example, the Big Three's 70 percent share of the American car and light-truck market). Moreover, investment in research, plant, and equipment is strong, productivity is high, and there are overseas operations and exporting. The secondary sector has the opposite characteristics. Revenues in an industry are spread across many small, not very profitable firms, their capital investment is low, and if they export it is indirectly, by supplying core-sector companies. The oligopolistic conditions in the core sector thus contrast with the highly competitive markets of the secondary sector.

This approach, then, maintains that the dual labor markets converge with the two economic sectors. The core sector includes the primary labor market, and the peripheral sector includes the secondary labor market. Employment in the primary labor market generally offers better pay and benefits, greater job security, and promotion ladders within companies (Doeringer and Piore, 1971). Age, gender, and race are considered important characteristics that filter workers into one or the other labor market segment. These attributes affect people's chances of acquiring the human capital (education, training, skills) that opens the door to the primary labor force.

Dual labor market theory provides some clues to wage differences, but it also has problems. Certainly, some industries are far more fragmented than others; larger firms, especially in more concentrated industries, do offer better pay and benefits; and human capital eases or obstructs access to jobs. The sectors, however, are much less clearly bounded than the theory suggests. When Hall (1994) drew together studies that classified industries as core or periphery, there was agreement on the classification of some industries and disagreement on others. Classifying an entire industry too often misses the mix of large and small companies. Still, even if there were agreement on the location of an industry in the core or the periphery, what would this currently mean?

The concept of oligopoly is difficult to defend when markets are as open as they are in the United States. Into the 1970s, a few major corporations in each key product line accounted for a large share of the U.S. market for cars, steel, oil, electrical equipment, chemicals, breakfast foods, commercial aircraft, synthetic fibers, soap, lightbulbs, and so on. The "competing" firms maintained comfortable profit margins by quietly agreeing not to compete too vigorously by undercutting one another's market prices (Reich, 1992, ch. 4). That description is no longer realistic. Even with a 70 percent share of the domestic market, General Motors, Ford, and Chrysler cannot set the terms for prices and quality because European and Japanese companies are eager and able to attract customers to their own vehicles. When the current rules of competition are not locally determined, practices in the core sector are fundamentally altered.

General Electric has halved its workforce since 1980, and a long list of other large corporations have made massive job reductions in recent years. IBM, Digital Equipment, and Kodak, American companies known for their internal career ladders and no-firing policies, abandoned these arrangements when foreign competitors gained substantial shares of the U.S. market. A large corporation is certainly unlikely to shut down completely, but it may trim its labor force, move parts of its operations elsewhere in the country or overseas, purchase some products and services previously supplied within the company, enter into joint ventures, or sell or merge business units. Thus the advantages of working in the core sector have been considerably lessened. Dual labor market theory does point to important influences on compensation, but it exaggerates the differences between labor market sectors.

Fourth, explanations of income based on the concept of *comparable worth* are directed at reducing unfair pay differences between male and female workers. The argument is along these lines: Legally defensible policies must be used to sort jobs for pay purposes. In small firms pay often reflects the prevailing community standards for comparable jobs, but in mid- to large-size companies more complicated techniques must be applied. The board of directors is responsible for setting executive compensation; below that level, a system of *job evaluation* is needed.

A widely applied, seemingly objective, method of job evaluation is the *point system,* organized around categories of jobs and subfactors which describe the content of jobs or the requirements to perform them. The following categories and subfactors are often used:

1. Skill: job knowledge, experience, initiative.
2. Effort: physical, visual, mental.

3. Responsibility: equipment or process, material or product, safety of others, work of others.
4. Working conditions: temperature, noise, hazards.

Each subfactor is divided into five or six levels, from low to high, and each is assigned a certain number of points. A low point value indicates that not much of that subfactor is needed or is present; a high point value indicates that to do the job the highest degree of that subfactor is needed or is present. Each category (skill, effort, and so on) is worth a certain number of points, as determined by the sum of the points for the subfactors jointly in it. Totaling all the points for all the categories provides an overall score that ranks jobs according to their comparative value to a firm.

This would be fine if points were in fact impartially assigned. Typically the rules for allocating points to subfactors within categories in job evaluation unfavorably affect the totals for jobs in which women are concentrated, even when the human capital requirements are the same (Steinberg, 1992). For instance, in the skill category, the maximum points for experience and initiative are larger than those for other subfactors, and the jobs women typically hold do not tend to score high on experience and initiative. The concept of comparable worth has been proposed to achieve the gender-neutral assignment of points for job content among different jobs (England, 1992). Though the law requires that persons in the *same* job must receive equal pay, people performing *different* tasks in a company are not currently shielded from prejudicial job evaluation systems.

These four theories offer useful clues to income distribution. Because historical time and place are involved, a grand, inclusive explanation will remain elusive.

Data on Income Distribution

Full-time workers' occupations and median weekly earnings in the United States are shown in Table 3–11. As expected, the top earners are executives, managers, and professionals, followed by technical workers. At the low end of the earnings scale are private household workers, farm workers, and "other service workers." Women consistently earn less than men in the same occupations. In these broad occupational categories, women tend to be in the lower-paying jobs— among professionals, for example, they are more often nurses and teachers than doctors or professors. Although these earnings disparities were greater in past years (Reskin and Padavic, 1994), women's median income for "all occupations" (bottom part of Table 3–11) is still

Table 3–11
Occupations and Median Weekly Earnings of Full-Time Workers,
United States, 1995

Occupational Category	Median Weekly Earnings		
	Men	Women	All Full-Time Workers
Executives, managers	$837	$577	$686
Professional specialty	844	623	722
Technicians	643	492	576
Sales	588	322	458
Clerical	485	386	400
Private household workers	NA	174	176
Protective services	569	431	544
Other service workers	295	261	274
Precision production, craft, and repair	519	369	509
Operators and fabricators	418	294	367
Helpers and laborers	320	286	314
Farming, forestry, and fishing	292	251	285
All occupations	533	404	475
By race or Hispanic origin			
White	562	412	491
Black	407	354	380
Hispanic	342	307	327

Sources: U.S. Department of Labor, Bureau of Labor Statistics, "Usual Weekly Earnings of Wage and Salary Workers: Second Quarter 1995," *News,* July 27, 1995, Tables 3, 4.

under 80 percent of men's. While for blacks and Hispanics women's average earnings are almost 90 percent of men's, that is due to the low wages of the men.

Comparing income in any one year can reveal relative advantage or disadvantage, but it is also important to know whether earnings are moving up or down. To get at that, comparisons over time are needed, and they must not disregard change in the value of money—its purchasing power. Incomes in "current" (face-value) dollars may be rising, but if the inflation rate is taken into account, those increases may shrink or even disappear. Using *real dollars* (also called "constant dollars") is a method for dealing with this. In Table 3–12, the column on the right uses 1983 dollars as the reference year for 1995 earnings. This means that the amount of inflation as measured by the Consumer Price Index (CPI) between 1983 and 1995 is subtracted from the 1995 income.[4] For example, the top row of Table 3–12 indicates that the income of execu-

---

[4]The Consumer Price Index is revised monthly by the U.S. Department of Labor, Bureau of Labor Statistics. The index is based on the retail prices of goods and services, including housing, transportation, food and beverages, clothing, and medical care.

Table 3–12
**Occupations and Median Weekly Earnings of Full-Time Workers,
United States, 1983 and 1995, and Real Median Weekly Earnings (1983 dollars)**

Occupational Category	Median Weekly Earnings 1983	1995	Real Weekly Earnings 1995
Executives, managers	$456	$686	$450
Professional specialty	422	722	473
Technicians	357	576	378
Sales	305	458	300
Clerical	258	400	262
Private household workers	111	176	115
Protective services	350	544	357
Other services	194	274	180
Precision production, craft, and repair	379	509	334
Operators and fabricators	261	367	241
Helpers and laborers	244	314	206
Farming, forestry and fishing	200	285	187
All occupations	309	475	311
By race			
White	321	491	322
Black	257	380	250
By Hispanic origin	250	327	214
By gender			
Male	379	533	350
Female	252	404	265

Sources: U.S. Bureau of the Census, *Statistical Abstract of the U.S.: 1985*, p. 419; U.S. Department of Labor, Bureau of Labor Statistics, "Usual Weekly Earnings of Wage and Salary Workers: Second Quarter 1995," *News*, July 27, 1995, Tables 3, 4.

tives and managers was $456 per week in 1983 and $686 in 1995, a gain of 50 percent. The real weekly earnings in 1995, however, are almost identical to the 1983 current income. This is dismaying for workers in occupations that have hardly kept up with inflation, but the situation is bleaker for those in occupations that have fallen behind. Considering all occupations, real earnings in 1995 were about the same as a decade earlier.

Looking further back, Mishel and Bernstein (1993) examined average real weekly earnings from 1947 to 1991 among production and nonsupervisory workers, who make up 80 percent of the private-sector labor force. They noted that real income almost doubled by 1973 and then gradually eroded to slightly below that peak. Other data show that from 1990 to 1995, production and nonsupervisory workers' real hourly wages slipped a little further below the mid-1970s level ("Help Wanted," 1995).[5]

But such economic phenomena have multiple consequences, and a disadvantage to one sector can be an advantage elsewhere. Lack of income growth in the United States has contributed to flat *unit labor costs* (the compensation needed to produce a unit of output), thus attracting overseas producers to use this country as a manufacturing base for exports to Asia, Europe, and South America ("Secret Weapon," 1994). In contrast, in Britain, France, Canada, Germany, and Japan, where real wages rose by 10 to 20 percent in the 1980s, new jobs were not created ("Job Woes," 1994).[6]

While most Americans had stagnant or even falling incomes, others experienced just the opposite. The best-paid members of the U.S. labor force are star professional athletes and entertainers, partners in leading law firms, and medical specialists ("Who'll Get the Lion's Share?" 1992). Also soaring high above the average is the income of senior managers in major U.S. companies. In the mid-1990s, the average chief executive officer (CEO) of a big corporation received salary plus bonus and stock options worth nearly $4 million. A record was set when the CEO of the Walt Disney Company collected total compensation of $203 million in 1993. In that same year, Disney profits had fallen by over 60 percent, to around $300 million ("That Eye-Popping Executive Pay," 1994). Big earnings, in some instances, represent excellent leadership, but often they do not. In the 1980s, executives in mid- to large-size American companies saw their real compensation double. Only British executives prospered more, while German, French, and Japanese managers had smaller gains (Mishel and Bernstein, 1993). U.S. corporate boards of directors routinely gave little oversight to executives' pay, though there is currently momentum for doing so. Largely due to complaints from large institutional stockholders, a growing number of boards are tying CEO income to corporate performance. For those who deliver higher stock prices and profits, compensation can be enormous ("Deliver—or Else," 1995).

A look at family incomes in the United States is revealing. Though the marriage bond is shakier than it used to be, most people do get married.

---

[5]Unionized workers have been better compensated than nonunionized workers in the same occupations. Organized labor, however, represents a dwindling portion of employees in the United States (discussed in Chapter 4).

[6]With high unit labor costs and labor laws that make it difficult to discharge workers, employers in Western Europe are reluctant to hire new workers. Unemployment has therefore gone up, whereas the American unemployment rate has come down. One reason is that Americans will accept jobs that pay less than they earned previously, while Europeans opt more often to stay unemployed. West Europeans receive generous (by U.S. standards) unemployment compensation with no time limits and full medical benefits ("Job Woes," 1994), while Americans lose medical benefits, and unemployment insurance is ordinarily limited to six months.

As economic units, families may have more than one earner or none (80 percent have at least one earner, and about half have two). In these data, families are defined as persons related by marriage, blood, or adoption. This includes married-couples and families maintained by women or men without spouses. Family income includes current pay, pensions, Social Security, unemployment compensation, interest, dividends, and transfer payments such as welfare (excluded are non-money items, such as food stamps or Medicaid).

Median family income for 1950–1993 is shown in Table 3–13. In the decades following World War II, income grew impressively, but the growth is less impressive when earnings are adjusted for inflation. The column on the right indicates that families' real incomes almost doubled between 1950 and 1970, but they have more or less stayed at that level since. In real dollars, then, family income, on average, has not improved in over two decades.

Two-earner families, however, have beat the average. The lower part of Table 3–13 indicates that when husband and wife both work, their joint incomes are far ahead of those of single-earner families.[7] On the

Table 3–13
Median Annual Family Income, United States, 1950–1993,
and Real Median Family Income (1983 dollars)

	Annual Family Income	Real Annual Family Income
1950	$ 3,319	$13,777
1960	5,620	18,956
1970	9,867	25,161
1975	13,719	25,398
1980	21,023	25,543
1983	24,580	24,580
1985	27,735	25,776
1987	30,970	27,262
1990	35,353	26,987
1993	36,959	25,577
1993 median annual income of:		
Families with just husband working	$29,380	
Families with husband and wife working	49,088	
Families maintained by women	20,436	

Sources: U.S. Bureau of the Census, *Statistical Abstract of the United States, 1984,* p. 463, and *1994,* p. 469; U.S. Department of Labor, Bureau of Labor Statistics, "Employment and Earnings Characteristics of Families: Fourth Quarter 1993," *News,* February 1, 1994, Table 10; and U.S. Bureau of the Census, *Income, Poverty, and Valuation of Noncash Benefits, 1993,* Current Population Reports, Series P60-188, Table D-2 (Washington, DC, 1995).

---

[7]Slightly under 18 percent of all families are maintained by single, widowed, or divorced women ("Employment and Earnings of Families," 1994).

Table 3–14
Money Income of Families, 1993, and Percent in Poverty,
by Race and Ethnicity, United States, 1960–1993

| | Percent of Families | | | | |
Annual Income	White	Black	Hispanic	Asian	All Families
Under $10,000	6%	26%	18%	9%	9%
$10,000–14,999	6	11	13	6	7
$15,000–24,999	14	19	21	11	16
$25,000–34,999	15	14	17	12	15
$35,000–49,999	19	13	14	20	19
$50,000–74,999	22	11	11	21	20
$75,000–99,999	9	4	4	11	8
$100,000 or more	9	2	2	10	6
Number (in millions)	52.5	8.0	5.9	1.7	68.5
Median income	$41,110	$21,542	$23,654	$43,418	$36,959
Percent in poverty					
1960	15%	48%	NA	NA	18%
1970	8	30	NA	NA	10
1980	8	29	23%	NA	10
1990	8	29	25	12%	11
1991	9	30	26	12	12
1992	9	31	26	12	12
1993	9	31	27	14	12

Note: Families are defined as living in poverty by the Social Security Administration index. In 1993 the poverty threshold for a family of four was $14,763. Money income for Asian families is shown for 1992. The "All Families" distribution of money income includes races not shown separately.

Sources: U.S. Bureau of the Census, *Statistical Abstract of the U.S., 1994*, pp. 49, 467, 479, 480, and *Money Income and Poverty Status of Families and Persons in the United States, 1980*, Current Population Reports, Series P60, no. 127, pp. 14, 15, 29 (Washington, DC, 1981); and *Income, Poverty, and Valuation of Noncash Benefits, 1993*, Current Population Reports, Series P60-188, Table D-2 (Washington, DC, 1995). 1993 data for Asian families in poverty was provided by the Bureau of the Census, Division of Income, Poverty, and Labor Force.

negative side for many employed wives is their "double shift" routine of work and home responsibilities. Most of the housework and child care continue to be done by women, without much help from their husbands (Presser, 1994; South and Spitze, 1994). Still, two-earner families, on average, are the best off; clearly the worst off are families maintained by women.

Distribution by Population Segments

Table 3–14 compares the incomes of population segments. Among lower-income families (under $15,000), there are markedly larger percentages of black and Hispanic families than others, while upper-income families ($75,000 plus) include substantially higher percentages of white and Asian families than others. These distributions are reflected in the bottom part of the table, which shows that nearly half of all black families were living in poverty at the start of the 1960s. Over the next 10 years, however, the proportions of poor families sharply dropped. Though poverty rates have not moved much since then, they began to notch up in the 1990s.

The steep decline of poverty in the 1960s is not likely to be repeated soon. Poverty rates could be cut through the private sector or public programs, but if the past several decades are a guide to the future, reasonably livable wages for unskilled work will not be generated by the private sector. Programs financed by the public purse are equally unlikely to significantly diminish poverty. Stagnant or sagging real incomes, along with shaky job security, have focused middle-class taxpayers' concerns on their own problems. There would surely be loud objections to policies that elevate the size or scope of transfer payments—welfare, for instance, or subsidized private-sector jobs.

Although real family incomes have stayed flat since the 1970s, as we have shown, they are considerably higher than in the 1950s. However, we have not examined the concentration or relative shares of income received. If the total money income obtained by all families is considered as 100 percent, how is the 100 percent divided among families, or groupings of them? In Table 3–15 this is explained in terms of *quintiles*—fifths (or 20 percent)—of the total money income.[8] The first column, for instance, indicates that in 1947, the 20 percent of families with the smallest earnings (lowest fifth) received 5 percent of the total family income, while the 20 percent with the largest earnings (highest fifth) had over 40 percent. The quintiles for white and black families in 1947 (not shown) were quite similar to their 1980 patterns, so the shifts visible in the 1990s began in the eighties. In that period, both white and black families at the upper end of earnings expanded their shares, whereas families in the bottom quintiles experienced shrinking shares. (A decrease of share from, say, 5 to 4 percent represents a 20 percent drop in the income available to the families in a quintile.) Among black families, moreover, income became much more concentrated, with a larger share of the total family incomes going to those at the upper levels.

Yet this still understates the situation, because the quintiles have different cut-off limits. In 1992, for example, the upper cut-off limit for membership in the lowest fifth was $19,000 for white families and $7,500

---

[8]Table 3–15 gives data on family money income for all families and for black and white families. Comparable data for Hispanic and Asian families are not available.

Table 3–15
Money Income of Families—Percent of Aggregate Income Received by Each
Fifth and Highest 5 Percent of U.S. Families, 1947–1992

	All Families			White Families		Black Families	
	1947	1980	1992	1980	1992	1980	1992
Lowest Fifth	5%	5%	4%	6%	5%	4%	3%
Second Fifth	12	12	11	12	11	10	8
Third Fifth	17	17	16	17	16	16	15
Fourth Fifth	23	24	24	24	24	25	25
Highest Fifth	43	42	45	41	44	45	49
Top 5 percent	18	15	18	15	17	16	19

Sources: U.S. Bureau of the Census, *Historical Statistics of the United States, Colonial Times to 1970,*
Bicentennial Edition, Part I (Washington, DC, 1975), p. 293; *Money Income and Poverty Status of Families and Persons in the U.S., 1980,* Current Population Reports, Series P60, no. 127 (Washington, DC, 1981), p. 15; and *Statistical Abstract of the United States: 1994,* p. 470.

for black families. The second quintile had upper limits of $32,000 for white families and $15,600 for black families. At the upper end, among the top 20 percent, the lower limit for inclusion was $66,250 for whites and $44,200 for blacks. On average, then, comparatively well-off black families are less affluent than the comparable white families, and poorer black families have less income than needy white families.

In the 1980s, family income became more unequally distributed among all races. However, incomes were even more highly concentrated in the 1920s and 1930s (the data do not separate races), with 25 to 30 percent of aggregate family earnings going to the top 5 percent (U.S. Bureau of the Census, 1975, p. 301). Federal taxes also took far smaller bites; until 1913, tariffs and business taxes provided enough to pay all the national government's bills, and there was no personal income tax. Income tax rates spiked up in the 1950s and 1960s, then drifted down. Effective tax rates—the amount of income, after adjustments, that is actually paid in taxes—now differ by a moderate 10 to 20 percent between families with higher or lower incomes, even with state and local taxes added (Reich, 1992, ch. 16). This has contributed to much wider differences in wealth (assets such as stocks, bonds, real estate). The richest 1 percent of America's families own almost 40 percent of the country's wealth. The highest 20 percent hold over 80 percent, a considerably larger share than in any other industrialized nation ("Gap in Wealth," 1995).

Based on the first decades after World War II, Americans had come to expect a steadily advancing standard of living. From the 1970s on, however, less benign circumstances became familiar. We return to America's economic dilemmas in Chapter 5.

Prestige

Prestige, often described as social standing, status, or respect, indicates location in a social hierarchy. The emergence of city-states and empires (see Chapter 1) introduced rigid social layering, or stratification, which became the usual social pattern for the next 5,000 years. India's ancient (and partially lingering) caste system, the aristocrat–free person–slave ranks of antiquity, the noble-commoner-serf distinctions of the Middle Ages are all examples. Not until the 1860s were feudal titles and privileges abolished in Japan, serfdom ended in Russia, and slaves freed in America.

Birth dictated social location in these systems. To use the terminology of sociology, rank was based on *ascription* (assigned) rather then *achievement* (earned). In the industrialized societies of the modern world, however, birth is viewed as a starting point from which unfavorable circumstances can be overcome.

The key social measure of achievement is occupation. Donald Treiman (1977) noted that differences in occupational prestige result from variations in control over scarce resources. These include (1) the *knowledge or skill* required for socially valued tasks, (2) *control* over economic resources on which others depend, and (3) the *authority* to coordinate or define others' work. Disparities in power are thus embedded in the division of labor, and power underpins prestige. Treiman went a step further, proposing that elite occupations in one country also will be highly regarded elsewhere: "the connections between educational requirements, income and prestige are similar throughout the world" (p. 115). Other analysts agree that education and income are the best predictors of occupational prestige (Erikson and Goldthorpe, 1993).

The surveys of the National Opinion Research Center (NORC) on occupational prestige have found consistent rankings over the years (Davis and Smith, 1993). It is not surprising that physicians and other professions are ranked at the top, skilled workers and technicians around the middle, and unskilled occupations at the bottom. However, Bose and Rossi (1983) give this type of research an interesting twist. Along with the conventional occupations ranked in their study, three nonpaying roles were included—housewife, househusband, and "person living on welfare." Housewife was ranked in the middle, househusband among the lower scores, and living on welfare nearly at the bottom.

Social judgments of occupations and alternative sources of livelihood have consequences. Internal effects bear on self-esteem; external effects involve relations with others. A core sociological principle is that people see themselves the way they think others see them. A personal circle of friends or relatives might respect a person for having a pleasant personality or being reliable, but local reputation can only soften, not displace, the broader social evaluations grounded in how the person earns a living. Low social standing, then, can result in low self-regard (Sennet and Cobb, 1973; Lewis, 1993).

The external impact on social relations is also significant. For example, the choice of a marriage partner from among potential mates is far from random. In addition to age, race, and religion, a social layering effect is visible. Men and women with similar aspirations and educational credentials usually find each other (Western and Wright, 1994). Baxter (1994) studied dual-earner couples in the United States, Sweden, Norway and Australia, examining the correspondence between the occupational levels of husbands and wives (six levels were used in this research). Over 50 percent of American couples were at the same level, and most of the rest were in an adjacent rank. The proportions were similar for couples in the other three countries.

Neighborhoods, too, tend toward homogeneity, housing families of roughly similar status and income (Reich, 1992, ch. 23). An important consequence is that children's futures are affected. In wealthier areas, many youngsters attend private schools, and going on to college is common; in the inner city, many of them attend rundown, sometimes dangerous schools in which the dropout rate is high, and continuing on to college is neither prepared for nor encouraged. Though a school's staff and physical resources are important to school achievement, so are the students. As parents know, and the classic study of Coleman and his colleagues (1966) confirms, adolescents strongly influence each other's responses to schooling.

These situations reflect a *class* form of stratification. Judgments are anchored in the outlook that occupation is not predestined by birth, effort can overcome disadvantages, and as Lewis (1993, p. 8) observes, "it is the individual alone who is socially significant...and who is therefore responsible for the degree of personal success achieved." The contest is pictured as open to all, so falling short may bring a sense of inadequacy, while getting ahead can bolster self-confidence.

Job Satisfaction

The third work outcome we will consider is job satisfaction, or work satisfaction. (These terms are used interchangeably in the literature on job outcomes, and we will use them both here, too.) The number of studies on work satisfaction reaches into the thousands. Much of the interest has focused on three issues: the link between satisfaction and productivity; the degree of job satisfaction among members of the labor force; and the connection between satisfaction and occupational or organizational characteristics.

Job Satisfaction and Productivity

Systematic research on job satisfaction and job performance can be traced to the famous Hawthorne studies of 1927–1932, conducted at the Western Electric Company's Hawthorne Plant in Chicago. The first studies had produced a totally unexpected finding. Lighting was increased and decreased in three departments, but no consistent link with productivity emerged. One department was then divided into a test group and control group. Lighting for the test group was increased and decreased, but it was kept constant for the control group. Productivity in the test group went up as illumination increased; surprisingly, it rose equally in the control group. Another two groups were then set up, and again the productivity of both groups increased. This led to more and broader studies, until funding stopped.

By the end of the 1930s the researchers' results were published (Roethlisberger and Dickson, 1939; Whitehead, 1939; Roethlisberger, 1941). Among the conclusions were:

1. Behavior should not be viewed as motivated primarily by economic or rational considerations. Rather, values, beliefs, and emotions largely influence actions.
2. Groups within organizations are the carriers of values and norms. Because people value their relationships in work groups, they powerfully affect behavior.
3. Organizations gain members' cooperation by satisfying them. The basis of satisfaction is membership in a cohesive, supportive work group.
4. A satisfied employee will be more productive.

These principles launched the field of human relations, which emphasizes the interactions within and between groups and the characteristics of tasks. If these elements satisfy people's needs, work effort will be energized. Specifically, the *relationships* within work groups should be supportive and cohesive, the relations between supervisors and employees should be collegial and nonauthoritarian, and *tasks* should provide opportunities for growth and autonomy (McGregor, 1957; Herzberg, 1968; Maslow, 1965).

The human relations perspective directly contradicted the theory and practice of scientific management, discussed in Chapter 2. Its advocates insisted that the motivational key to higher productivity was the pay envelope (Taylor, 1947/1911). Work-group members, according to scientific management, were naturally concerned with restricting output in order to protect themselves against higher production standards for the same wage. The solution was to offer a tangible incentive for productivity.

Singly or in combination, these views continue to provide the themes for explanations of job satisfaction and productivity. Individuals are viewed as responsive to the material benefits (*extrinsic rewards*) of their work, to its psychological stimuli (*intrinsic rewards*), or to both.

Roethlisberger and Dickson's influential report *Management and the Worker* (1939) promoted the idea that productivity is tied to employee satisfaction. While at first glance this may seem reasonable, research has not supported the satisfaction-effort correlation. Curiously, the original Hawthorne data can be interpreted as showing weak or no association (Parsons, 1974; Carey, 1967). Since the researchers could not agree on what the data proved, the experiments' funding and leadership apparently swayed the published conclusions (Gillespie, 1991). As early as the 1950s, a review of research on morale and productivity had concluded that "there is little evidence in the available literature that employee attitudes of the type usually measured in morale surveys bear any simple—or for that matter, appreciable—relationship to performance on the job" (Brayfield and Crockett, 1955, p. 408). Ever since, weak associations have been reported (Vroom, 1964; Ronan, 1970; Steers and Porter, 1987).

The link, in fact, is not necessarily obvious. In survey after survey, Japanese workers report lower work satisfaction than their Western counterparts (Lincoln and McBride, 1987). A large-scale study by Lincoln and Kalleberg (1990) directly compared Japanese and American workers, again with the same results. Considering these satisfaction measures, perhaps American workers outdo Japanese workers' productivity and quality, but these researchers make no such claim. What, then, is going on? Lincoln and Kalleberg explain that Japanese workers, regardless of satisfaction levels, have a robust sense of obligation to do the work as best they can. The feeling of duty (buttressed by job security and profit-sharing) is thus central to these workers' behavior. Others have also pointed out that Japanese workers' gripes about their bosses and companies are not reflected in work performance (Kamata, 1982, pp. vii–xl; Katzenstein, 1989).

Thus it appears that satisfaction is a dubious predictor of behavior on the job. Nonetheless, analysts have found that *intentions* do relate to actions (Pinder, 1984, ch. 8; Robbins, 1994). A general attitude (such as satisfaction) is of slight help in predicting a broad behavior (such as work effort), but narrowly specified intentions can reasonably well predict specific actions. For instance, if a coworker says she wants to improve her job skills, what can be predicted? Not much. But if she says, beginning next week, she will learn computer programming, and she'll sign up tomorrow for the appropriate class, we could predict with some assurance that she will follow through. Specific intentions attached to clearly specified actions result in firmer connections. The managerial practices of management by objectives and goal setting take advantage of this intention-action relation (Robbins, 1994).

Another link between attitude and behavior can be seen when a distinction is made between (1) the motivation to exert more effort or less effort at work and (2) the motivation to remain in an organization or escape it through absences or quitting. Level of satisfaction is a weak predictor of (1) but a stronger predictor of (2). Workplace pressures limit uncooperative actions by employees. Performance standards and expectations (including their own), performance reviews, pay and promotion decisions, and potential job references constrain such overt behavior, but absenteeism and quitting are other forms of noncooperation or withdrawal of effort. So while satisfied workers may not be more productive, the evidence indicates that they will decrease absenteeism and turnover in the firm (Mowday, Porter, and Steers, 1982; Martin and Miller, 1986; Lawler, 1990). Still, discontent does not necessarily prod retreat from work situations. A worker may want to get out of a displeasing situation but believe that the results could be even worse—frequent absences could lead to loss of the job, and quitting without an alternative in hand is risky. Satisfaction-dissatisfaction thus joins other concerns that also influence absenteeism and turnover.

The attitude-behavior relationship is by no means simple. Satisfaction with intrinsic rewards will not by itself sustain higher levels of effort. The combination of intrinsic and extrinsic rewards, however, constitutes an effective set of incentives. High-performance work sites (discussed in Chapter 5) offer a package of incentives. Finally, there is an interesting twist in the commonly weak link between satisfaction and performance. Among service jobs that involve *direct* customer/client contact (salesclerk, insurance agent, flight attendant, dentist), the provider's attitude, as reflected in his or her demeanor, is critical. A surly waiter may bring a diner a fine meal, but the customer will not revisit that restaurant. Attitudinal signals that are petty in behind-the-scenes work are key aspects of performance in contact situations (Kanter, 1993). Of course, attitude can be manipulated. Frontline workers know that a friendly, caring orientation attracts customers. Many businesses—fast food, insurance, airlines—monitor and train direct-contact personnel for suitably pleasing conduct (Leidner, 1993).[9]

The Distribution of Work Satisfaction

Job or work satisfaction has most often been measured with one of two methods. One seeks to assess overall or *global satisfaction*. Survey respondents are asked to judge their total work experience by answering a question such as: "All things considered, how satisfied are you with your job?" They choose from alternatives that range from "highly satisfied" to "highly dissatisfied." The other method centers on facets of the job. Respondents are given a list of items such as "the work is interesting," "the job security is good," "the pay is good," "the physical surroundings are pleasant." For each item they select from options that range from "very true" to "not at all true."

Replies to a global work satisfaction question in a National Opinion Research Center (NORC) survey are shown in Table 3–16. Employed persons were asked: "On the whole, how satisfied are you with the work you do—would you say you are very satisfied, moderately satisfied, a little dissatisfied, or very dissatisfied?" Though a small decrease of "very satisfied" responses can be seen over the years, more than 80 percent of workers surveyed in the 1990s said they had favorable (very or moderately satisfied) opinions about their jobs. In these nationally representative samples, the NORC included a related question: "If you were to get enough money to live as comfortably as you would like for the rest of your life, would you continue to work or would you stop working?" Seven out of ten men and women said they would continue to work, and this rate has hardly budged over the years (Davis and Smith, 1993, p. 238). These endorsements of work and working invite the conclusion that workers who say they are satisfied with their jobs are in fact pleased. The response, nevertheless, is more ambiguous.

If satisfaction is probed with a different sort of question, larger proportions of people express negative feelings. When respondents are asked whether or not they would choose the same kind of work they are

---

[9]A display of suitable attitudes is also crucial for managers. Regardless of actual sentiments toward the boss's assignments, an optimistic, can-do disposition usually finds favor. Jackall (1988) found that opportunistic self-presentation is considered necessary for career advancement. Kanter (1993) reports similar findings.

Table 3–16
Responses to NORC Surveys on Work Satisfaction, 1972–1994

Response Categories	Percent of Responses			
	1972–1982	1983–1987	1988–1991	1993–1994
Very satisfied	50%	48%	47%	46%
Moderately satisfied	36	37	40	41
A little dissatisfied	9	10	9	10
Very dissatisfied	4	4	4	3
Don't know or no answer	1	1	–	–
Total	100%	100%	100%	100%
Number of respondents	7,947	4,681	3,542	2,978

Source: Data calculated from James A. Davis and Tom Smith, *General Social Surveys, 1972–1994: Cumulative Code Book* (Chicago: National Opinion Research Center, 1994), p. 188.

presently doing if they could start their work lives again, the "no" answers range from 10 percent of professionals to 80 percent of unskilled workers. All in all, almost half of the respondents said that another line of work would be more appealing (Kahn, 1974; Hodson and Sullivan, 1995). This approach thus registers people's discontent with their work.

Admitting dissatisfaction implies an inability to hold a more favorable job. Moreover, cultural values may inhibit a negative view of one's work. Explaining why Japanese and German workers consistently report lower satisfaction than Americans, Lincoln and Kalleberg (1990, p. 51) comment that "cultural pressures in the U.S. induce individuals to color positively their reports of job experiences."

Although variations in global satisfaction are in fact measurably related to occupations, the relationship is rather feeble. Table 3–17 indicates that the responses of professionals, managers, and skilled workers diverge from those of workers in semiskilled and unskilled jobs. Among the less skilled, fewer people say they are very satisfied and more that they are discontented, yet nearly 8 out of 10 are in the satisfied camp. The dissatisfaction rates are quite low.

An important question is whether such characteristics as gender, race, ethnicity, or age affect work satisfaction. The data underlying Table 3–17 (not shown), for example, indicate that they barely sway opinions about jobs. Indeed, the general answer is no, but some studies have found that these characteristics do have consequences for satisfaction (Hall, 1994).

One other explanation of favorable work attitudes is the *fit hypothesis*, which suggests that satisfaction is based on the match between a job's attributes—pay, skill requirements, status and so on—and the worker's circumstances (Hodson and Sullivan, 1995). For instance, we would

Table 3–17
Responses to NORC Survey on Work Satisfaction, by Occupation, 1993/1994
(in percent)

Response Categories	Occupational Category						
	Professional and Technical	Managerial	Sales	Clerical	Services	Skilled Jobs	Semiskilled and Unskilled Jobs
Very satisfied	58%	52%	44%	41%	42%	46%	31%
Moderately satisfied	33	38	42	43	41	42	48
A little dissatisfied	7	7	10	12	11	9	17
Very dissatisfied	2	3	3	4	6	3	4
Don't know or no answer	–	–	1	–	–	–	–
Total	100%	100%	100%	100%	100%	100%	100%
Number of respondents	630	356	362	496	406	284	373

Source: Data calculated from James A. Davis and Tom Smith, *General Social Surveys, 1972–1994, Cumulative Code Book* (Chicago: National Opinion Research Center, 1994), p. 188.

expect discontent among college-graduates in jobs for which they are overqualified (say, retail sales). But if they have recently graduated from college, unemployment is high, and they regard the work as only temporary until more suitable employment comes along, their opinions may tip toward satisfaction.

The fit approach proposes that people respond to jobs in light of their *human capital* (education, skills, experience), *characteristics* (age, gender, race), *situation* (family to support, for instance), and *conditions* in the job market (in general and specifically). With a quick mental summary of these factors, most workers report that "All things considered, my job is okay." Of course, this could also be understood as an accommodation to a less-than-perfect reality. Since when people are asked whether they would choose their current line of work again, many say they would not, it seems that they can be simultaneously satisfied and discontented.[10] That is, workers may be satisfied overall, given the market for their particular education, skills, and experience, yet dissatisfied with specific features of their jobs.

What do people want from their work? Analysts' answers have varied over time. In the 1950s and 1960s, human relations theory was popular. Supportive groups, interesting work, and involvement in decisions

---

[10]Frederick Herzberg (1968), an influential human relations theorist, also thought that individuals can be simultaneously satisfied and dissatisfied. Herzberg had in mind that satisfaction is the result of intrinsic rewards, whereas dissatisfaction is related to extrinsic factors. Our emphasis, however, is on satisfaction and discontent at different layers of judgment about one's job.

were what employees "really" wanted. Earlier, and again later, economic incentives were thought to be primary. The current and most realistic viewpoint is that both intrinsic and extrinsic rewards are important in work (Lawler, 1990; Pinchot and Pinchot, 1993).

This approach is supported by the NORC data, collected for over two decades. On a scale of 1 (unimportant) to 7 (important), three out of four respondents chose either a 6 or 7 for both types of rewards (Davis and Smith, 1993, pp. 238–44). Most workers thus prefer some degree of complexity and variety in their work, meaningful tasks with a dose of autonomy, and involvement with others in doing their jobs. But they also want good pay and benefits, steady work, advancement opportunities and safe working conditions. Some jobs come closer than others to meeting these preferences. This largely explains the persistent differences in satisfaction among occupations, and the low-skill workers who wish they could restart their work lives. Means of improving work outcomes are discussed in Chapter 4.

SUMMARY

The U.S. civilian labor force included over 130 million persons in the mid-1990s. Men's participation rates have been relatively stable for a century, whereas women's participation rates have sharply increased over the last 50 years. In nearly half of all American families, both the husband and wife hold jobs.

People are connected to their work by its results for them. There are numerous outcomes, though the major ones are pay, prestige, and job satisfaction. Following steep gains after World War II, real earnings stalled. In response to imports that captured a growing share of the U.S. market, American companies began downsizing and restructuring in the 1980s. Stagnant incomes and anxieties about jobs became stubborn realities for many American families.

Occupations, and alternatives such as welfare, are socially evaluated, and judgments about how one makes a living have significant consequences for relationships and self-esteem. Marriage partners often have similar educations, and if both work they are likely to be in roughly the same occupational tier. Among individuals at the low end of work achievement, however, self-confidence may waver.

The concept of job or work satisfaction has drawn enormous attention among theorists, stimulated by the belief that satisfaction and productivity are directly linked. Lacking empirical support, this view gave way to the current one that both intrinsic and extrinsic factors influence job performance, and most workers apparently do want both. Managers, professionals, and skilled workers report higher satisfaction than other workers, but only a minority of Americans in any occupation say they are dissatisfied. Puzzled observers have offered several explanations to account for such widespread optimistic responses.

4   Changing Work Outcomes

A large portion of many people's lives is invested in work. American culture encourages work, and economic necessity ordinarily demands it. Preserving and improving work outcomes, therefore, is a central interest from executive suite to shop floor.

Since decreased results are frustrating, whereas gains are welcomed, competition over work outcomes among individuals and groups should be expected. Two forms of this competition—individual occupational mobility and collective actions by labor unions—are discussed in this chapter. Collaboration in the workplace is discussed in Chapter 5.

OCCUPATIONAL MOBILITY

The concept of occupational mobility involves movement up or down among occupational categories. It may be intragenerational, focused on workers' careers throughout life, or intergenerational, concerned with shifts across generations.

Intragenerational Mobility and Labor Turnover

Intragenerational occupational mobility (also called career or worklife mobility) refers to occupational shifts within a person's working life. Mobility may be upward to a better job, downward to a worse job, or lateral (outcomes stay the same). An aspect of *occupational mobility* that results from both workers' and employers' actions is *labor turnover*, the separations from a firm brought on by quits and layoffs and the accessions to it, including new hires.

The amount of turnover in the American economy is fairly high. One reason is that many young persons who enter the labor force often start in jobs that happen to be available and then seek more advantageous positions (Krecker, 1994). Others, of course, may prefer another job or no job, for a variety of reasons, such as job dissatisfaction, commuting distance, shift work, childbearing and rearing, or retirement. And many firms scale employment up or down in response to the demand for their products or services.

Government surveys on labor turnover for 1993 show that in any given month, about 4 percent of the labor force was not working due to layoffs or the end of temporary jobs, and 1 percent was unemployed because workers had quit their jobs (U.S. Department of Labor, 1994). In that same year, employers added to their payrolls nearly 2.5 million new hires. The annual *labor turnover rate* (the net voluntary and involuntary job separations and hiring, relative to total employment) is higher in the U.S. than in Western Europe; Japan has the least turnover (Freeman, 1994).

What happens after Americans lose their jobs? Between January 1991 and December 1993, 9 million full-time wage earners became unemployed. As of early 1994, 66 percent had found new employers, 20 percent were unemployed (but half of the older workers), and the rest had dropped out of the labor force. Among those with new employment, about 25 percent earned much less than before, another 25 percent earned substantially more, and the other 50 percent was close to previous earnings ("Worker Displacement," 1994).

As the turnover rate has increased over the decades, *job tenure*, the average length of time that employees work for the same employer, has gone down. In the 1950s people changed jobs about seven times during a lifetime, not counting those they had while in school (Lipset and Bendix, 1959); now the average number of moves is closer to nine. But individuals not only change employers, they also switch occupations; each year about 10 percent of workers make such a change. At least one change in occupation over the working years is common ("Employee Tenure," 1992).

In the 1970s, among workers who changed jobs and occupations in a given year, the net result was upward mobility (U.S. Department of Labor, 1980). At about the same time, other studies that traced job changers over a longer period (from first job after completing their education to the time of the survey) similarly reported that the net effects were upward movement (Hauser and Featherman, 1977; Stern and Johnson, 1968). For instance, using a five-tier occupational classification to examine American men's worklife mobility, upward exceeded downward movement by 25 percent (Haller et al., 1985). While women's mobility rates were about the same, the income results were weaker, due to sex-segregated employment (Reskin and Padavic, 1994). The margin of upward over downward mobility for both men and women then began to shrink as employment opportunities and relationships changed.

In the 1980s, competitive pressures from the growing global economy jolted American corporations. Companies began to invest heavily in production and communication technologies that facilitate organizational and workforce restructuring. Among the results were a movement of jobs to lower wage areas of the United States or overseas, and job cuts that included middle managers and professionals. The manufacturing sector's share of employment continued to decline, while the service-sector continued to expand, bolstering the employment trend toward more low-skilled, low-wage jobs. This mischievous combination of circumstances narrowed opportunities for upward intragenerational mobility ("Job Drought," 1992; Hout, 1988).

Intergenerational Mobility

Intergenerational mobility refers to shifts in occupations across generations, such as by fathers and sons. For reasons explained later, mobility research has given males the most attention. The concept of intergenerational mobility centers on vertical movement—upward to a more highly rewarded occupation, or downward. If the shift between *origin* (occupation of father or, sometimes, his social class) and *destination* (the offspring's current job) involves occupations with equivalent rewards, this horizontal pattern is considered "no movement." Studies of intergenerational mobility have concentrated on these questions: Is there as much upward and downward mobility now as in earlier years? What are the patterns of movement between occupational origins and destinations? And what are the variables that explain intergenerational mobility?

Analysts have largely agreed that two main processes underlie intergenerational mobility (Lipset and Bendix, 1959; Erikson and Goldthorpe, 1993):

1. New occupations may be created or existing ones multiplied. If the pool of newly generated jobs includes a larger proportion of highly rewarded positions than less well-rewarded ones, the opportunities for upward mobility are greater.
2. If access to new or existing positions is based on achieved rather than ascribed criteria, mobility opportunities are expanded.

Industrialized societies foster occupational mobility in both these ways. The growth of white-collar occupations and the decline of ascription (birth status as a determinant of occupational placement) have been the broad trends, although some groups have been less affected by them than others. Compared to white men, proportionately fewer American black men and women or white women have had the credentials to open the doors to higher-level occupations, or if they attain the credentials, they have not gotten past the gatekeepers as readily. While this situation has substantially improved, it has not been entirely eliminated. Researchers have found several variables that are especially useful in explaining mobility.

Explanations of Intergenerational Mobility

Featherman and Hauser's (1978) research on intergenerational mobility was based on a national sample of nearly 21,000 men between 20 and 64 years of age in the early 1970s. Analysis showed that higher placement on several measures—sons' education, and fathers' occupations and education—had the strongest positive impacts on mobility, whereas the chances were lessened by farm origins and large families. Among black sons, the findings differed only slightly.[1]

Education was the single most potent variable in this study of occupational mobility, regardless of skin color. Featherman and Hauser compared their findings with a similar early-1960s study and found that education had become considerably more important for occupational placement by the 1970s. Moreover, comparisons among age groups in the later survey showed that in the youngest group (age 25–34), the link between education and occupation among black males was nearly as strong as it was among their white age-peers. For older black men (age 55–64), education had a much weaker effect than among their white counterparts. These findings indicate that the tie between schooling and occupational advancement had become visibly stronger among black men. Ascription, in short, was in retreat.

The major elements found to affect mobility are listed below. Researchers ("Symposium," 1992) point to them as the important influences on the intergenerational mobility of offspring:

1. Education of offspring. Higher educational level raises occupational level.
2. Education of parents. Higher level enhances offsprings' occupational level.
3. Occupations of parents. Higher level improves offsprings' chances for upward mobility.

---

[1]Homes headed by divorced or single parents especially lowered black sons' mobility chances.

4. "Broken family." Families headed by single or divorced parents weaken mobility changes.
5. Number of siblings. Larger numbers of siblings reduce mobility chances.
6. Birth order. First or last child in family has better mobility chances.

The same variables used in the studies of fathers and sons have been used to statistically explain women's occupational placement. Put another way, for women and for men intergenerational mobility is similarly connected to origins (Hauser and Featherman, 1977; Erikson and Goldthorpe, 1993, ch. 7). Nevertheless, some fundamental issues remain. Less data are available on women, since most intergenerational mobility research has concentrated on men. Also, there is disagreement on just how women's mobility should be assessed, a problem to be described later.

Relating the occupational (or class) placement of one generation to another is conceptually and statistically complicated, so researchers' tactics differ. Three methodological practices, however, generally underlie this type of research:

1. The surveys ordinarily include only working-age respondents (21 to 64 years old).
2. Individuals are usually asked what their fathers' occupations were when the respondents were 16 years old, or in high school, or while growing up.
3. The number of origin/destination categories is not standardized; they vary from a few broad groupings to several dozen narrower categories.

Featherman and Hauser's (1978) findings from the early 1970s show much more upward than downward mobility—over twice as many sons had moved up than had slipped down. A decade later the pattern was different; data collected by the NORC in 1982 indicate that while there was still more upward (36 percent) than downward (26 percent) movement, it had slowed (Tausky, 1984, pp. 113–15). Another intergenerational mobility study using a national U.S. sample about the same time (Western and Wright, 1994) offers a look at sons' mobility from another angle, movement from blue-collar origins to white-collar destinations and vice versa. Considered that way, upward mobility to white-collar jobs exceeded downward mobility by a slim 6 percent.[2] Overall, then, the margin between upward and downward movement for men was shrinking.

---

[2]This is my calculation of Western and Wright's data (1994, pp. 626–27).

The basic issue in arguments over the measurement of women's occupational mobility (Erikson and Goldthorpe, 1993, ch. 7) is: How should the status (occupational destination) of an employed married woman be established? The variables may be (1) the wife's work, (2) the husband's work, (3) a combination of the husband's and wife's occupations, or (4) either the husband's or wife's occupation. In the first situation, status is considered an individual matter; in the second, the entire family's social location rests on the husband's employment. In the third view, both spouses' employment jointly determines the family's social location; in the fourth, it is determined by *either* the husband's or wife's work, depending on which one is the chief breadwinner. All these proposals reflect the fact that many wives have jobs, but which one best captures that reality is unclear.[3] In practice, most research uses the first method, centered on married women's occupations.

Several conclusions can be drawn from these studies. Men's and women's mobility is explained with the same factors; in linking origins and destinations, the strongest element is education. But women and men are not quite equal beneficiaries of higher levels of education, although the mobility rates are comparable if broad categories are used. For example, women professionals still are often in sex-segregated occupations—teachers, social workers, librarians, registered nurses—and women's entry into high-paying employment is limited by gender concentration in the workplace (Erikson and Goldthorpe, 1993; Roos, 1985).[4] Nevertheless, gains for American women may be expected. Women are earning a growing share of MBAs, CPAs and other professional degrees in fields that are mostly staffed by men.

Economic circumstances, of course, may intervene. In the years ahead, will too many qualified candidates be chasing after too few good jobs, or will ample openings be available? Both women's and men's advancement prospects are entangled in these developing conditions. Chapter 5 returns to this topic.

UNIONS AND COLLECTIVE BARGAINING

Worker organizations are either absent or government-controlled in many areas of the world—China and North Korea, for example, or the Persian Gulf OPEC countries. The former Soviet Union and most of its

---

[3]Marriage itself, of course, can affect intergenerational mobility. European studies consistently found that women's upward mobility rates through marriage equaled or exceeded men's (Erikson and Goldthorpe, 1993, p. 257).

[4]These studies note that in Europe and Japan, women's intergenerational mobility into well-paid employment is also less than men's. The reasons parallel those in the United States.

political allies formed essentially state-run labor organizations. Wherever governments are unelected—or if elected, the results are rigged—the development of any independent power base such as unions is obstructed. In contrast, political parties in North America and Western Europe are dependent on attracting electoral support, and the votes of workingmen and, later, their wives have proved helpful. Collective bargaining, originally viewed as criminal activity, came to be seen as lawful combined representation.

The Legal Framework

Throughout the 1800s, U.S. courts held that it was illegal for workers to band together for the purpose of negotiating with employers (Gould, 1993, ch. 2). These rulings were based on interpretations of "anticombination" statutes—originally directed at businesses—as being applicable to employees. Workers attempting to increase their wages by group action could face a criminal charge for entering into an unlawful conspiracy in restraint of trade. By the 1840s, the unlawful conspiracy doctrine, while not overturned, had become more uncertain. As an alternative defense against unions, employers raised the "tort" (civil) doctrine that inflicting intentional economic harm is illegal unless a legitimate goal justifies the harm. Since strikes and picketing are intended to cause economic losses, unions that used these tactics were at risk of liability for the economic injury they imposed on an employer. The concept of legitimate purpose was muddy, and it inspired a good deal of litigation. Court rulings were mostly, though inconsistently, unfriendly to union actions.

A surer legal remedy against worker organizations was provided in 1890 by the Sherman Antitrust Act. Aimed at attempts to stifle competition between firms, this act prohibited any contract or combination of business interests in restraint of foreign or domestic trade. Soon after it was passed, however, employers' arguments that the actions of worker organizations have the same result and are therefore illegal, began to be heard in the courts. The Sherman Antitrust Act proved to be an effective judicial safeguard against union activities.

A definitive case, *Danbury Hatters*, went to the Supreme Court in 1908. Workers had struck a hatmaker in hopes of unionizing the company. The issue before the Court hinged on whether antitrust legislation intended to prevent businesses from anticompetitive actions also applied to worker organizations. The Court decided that it did apply. Not only was forming a union now a potentially criminal action, but the Sherman Act allowed for triple punitive damages. Union members in the *Danbury Hatters* case were held personally liable for economic losses caused by the strike. The Supreme Court's ruling that the Sherman Antitrust Act included worker organizations allowed lower courts to dissolve "combinations." Unions and worker-organizing activities faced a grave threat.

Union supporters responded by vigorously campaigning for the Clayton Act, and its enactment in 1914 created the expectation that worker organizations had finally won judicial protection. This act stated:

> Nothing contained in the antitrust laws shall be construed to forbid the existence and operation of labor…organizations…or to forbid or restrain individual members from lawfully carrying out the legitimate objects thereof; nor shall such organizations, or the members thereof, be held or construed to be illegal combinations…in restraint of trade, under the antitrust laws. (Gould, 1993, p. 15)

The results of the Clayton Act, however, would disappoint its proponents—unions were still not shielded from judicial actions. The economic pressures that unions could properly use in a dispute were unclear. Lower courts found that although worker organizations as such are not illegal, their use of illegal tactics could be stopped by granting an injunction—a court order prohibiting a specific action. By the early 1930s, employers had obtained hundreds of injunctions to stop organizing activities, picketing, boycotts, and strikes. Moreover, the Supreme Court had ruled that the doctrine of conspiracy in restraint of trade applies to worker organizations when improper methods are used in a labor dispute (Levitan, 1961).

The pendulum swung in the other direction with enactment of the Norris-LaGuardia Act in 1932. The intent was to prevent the courts from overriding the will of Congress, as they had with previous legislation. The Norris-LaGuardia Act accomplished what the Clayton Act could not. Unions were now effectively guarded from federal injunctions. Nevertheless, state courts could still issue injunctions, and both federal and state courts remained free to hear civil suits against unions for violation of antitrust laws (Gold, 1989). This critical vulnerability was soon ended by the Supreme Court when it unambiguously ruled that the Norris-LaGuardia Act shields worker organizations from antitrust laws. The protection of union actions such as strikes and picketing, however, is only one among other obstacles to union growth. None of the legislation so far had prevented employers from discharging workers for joining a union or had required employers to bargain with a union even if it represented a majority of workers. Without these safeguards, employers could frustrate collective bargaining. Further legislation was needed.

The National Labor Relations Act (or Wagner Act) of 1935 established the framework of America's present union-management relations. The

Wagner Act integrated two goals: to specify permissible and not permissible behaviors in employer-union relations, and to create a mechanism for administering and enforcing those rules. It prohibits employers from either interfering with employees' rights to organize and bargain collectively or refusing to bargain with representatives of the employees. The act also details the procedures for employees to use in choosing their collective bargaining representatives. To apply these rules and methods, the act created the National Labor Relations Board, which is guided by the Wagner Act and two later acts, Taft-Hartley and Landrum-Griffin.

While the Wagner Act prohibited employers from taking specific actions, the Labor Management Relations Act of 1947 (often called the Taft-Hartley Act) added prohibitions of certain union activities. Passage of this act reflected the concern that the Wagner Act had not provided a balanced relationship between labor and management. The Taft-Hartley prohibitions on union activities (Anderson, 1980) include:

1. Attempting to cause an employer to discriminate against an employee because of membership or nonmembership in a labor organization, with the exception of union shop agreements,[5] whereas closed shop contracts are unlawful.
2. Refusing to bargain in good faith with an employer.
3. Encouraging employees to stop work in order to compel an employer to assign particular work to members of the union instead of members of another union (the jurisdictional strike).
4. Encouraging employees to stop work in order to compel an employer to stop doing business with another firm (the secondary boycott).

Unions had strongly opposed the passage of Taft-Hartley, voicing particular objections to the banning of the closed shop and the secondary boycott. The *closed shop* is a contractual agreement that requires an employer to hire only workers who are already members of the union. *Secondary boycotts* aim at firms that are indirectly connected to a labor dispute. Such secondary parties are buyers of a product or service provided by the primary employer. The goal of a secondary boycott is to exert economic pressure on the primary employer through loss of customers.

---

[5]Arrangements such as the closed shop and the union shop are called *union security agreements*. The *union shop* is a contractual provision that allows an employer to hire any worker, provided all new hires join the union within a specified time and remain members; otherwise the employer has to fire them. In an *agency shop*, an employee may choose not to join the union, although a fee must be paid to the union for its services. Twenty-one states have "right to work" laws which prohibit all such union security arrangements.

Union leaders feared that this combination of prohibitions would strip away important economic tools in labor disputes. The ban on closed shops was loosely enforced, however, and indirect methods for carrying out secondary boycotts were developed.

A dozen years after Taft-Hartley, passage of the Labor-Management and Disclosure Act (Landrum-Griffin Act) in 1959 was prompted by congressional hearings that had uncovered corrupt practices among a number of unions. Officials of the International Brotherhood of Teamsters were found to be especially shady, having developed ties with organized crime. Jack Barbash (1980), a long-time student of these matters, observed that "Much of the Landrum-Griffin Act was written against a legislative history of Teamster racketeering and internal repression" (p. 563). Exposed were such practices of the Teamsters Union and others as payments by employers to union officials to assure favorable wage agreements, labor peace (despite poor working conditions), or nonenforcement of some provisions of the contract (Aaron, 1967).

The Landrum-Griffin Act guarantees specific rights to union members and imposes certain obligations on union officers (Gould, 1993, ch. 4; Anderson, 1980). Among the obligations are that each labor organization must file its procedures and annual financial records with the U.S. secretary of labor, and this information must be disclosed to union members. Further, the act included a "bill of rights" giving union members:

1. Equal rights to attend and vote at meetings.
2. Protection from increases in dues except under specified procedures, for example, secret ballots at a meeting or mailed referendum.
3. The right to inspect collective bargaining agreements.
4. The guarantee of fair election of officers, including a reasonable opportunity to nominate candidates.

Landrum-Griffin, however, also prohibited unions from negotiating various contract provisions. Contract clauses are illegal if they (1) forbid handling "hot cargo" (goods from an employer engaged in a dispute with the union); (2) disallow an employer from subcontracting work out to nonunion employees; and (3) grant secondary boycotts.

The National Labor Relations Board

Collectively, the Wagner, Taft-Hartley, and Landrum-Griffin acts and amendments have been termed the *Labor Act* (Gold, 1989), and the National Labor Relations Board (NLRB) is responsible for administering it.[6] The Act's involvement in labor-management matters is derived from the interstate commerce clause of the U.S. Constitution. In effect, the Labor Act and therefore the NLRB apply to most persons working in the private sector. Specifically excluded from the Labor Act are: managers and supervisors; federal, state, and local public-sector (government) employees; employees of railroads or airlines; agricultural workers; independent contractors; domestic servants; and spouses and children of employers. In most cases, employees who are unprotected by the Labor Act are covered by state laws or other federal legislation.

The NLRB has two principal functions: to prevent and remedy unfair labor practices by employers or unions, and to conduct elections among employees to determine if they want to be represented by a union. Much hinges on the question: Who is an "employee"? The NLRB protects only the collective bargaining rights of persons defined as employees by the Labor Act. Excluded from protection, therefore, are *managers*, defined as persons who devise and execute company policy; and *supervisors*, individuals with authority to hire, fire, transfer, reward, and discipline or to effectively recommend such actions. In short, therefore, a person with authority over other employees is removed from NLRB protection. For instance, in the highly publicized *Yeshiva University* case, the NLRB ruled in 1980 that the faculty of the university exercised managerial authority in hiring, promotion, and other administrative matters (Douglas, 1994). The university, therefore, was not required to recognize the faculty union. (As discussed later, this case and others put at risk employee-involvement schemes.)

In Europe, a work unit can have several unions; whereas in the United States the Labor Act mandates "exclusivity." Only one labor organization can represent a bargaining unit. A union, moreover, must fairly represent all the workers in a bargaining unit, including those who choose not to join the union. The main criteria for forming a bargaining unit include shared working area, common supervision, similarity of job duties, interdependence of operations, and similar pay methods and rates. In the petition for holding an election, the union indicates the prospective members of the bargaining unit. If the union

---

[6]Various government agencies apply other laws that significantly affect the workplace (Gold, 1993; Gould, 1993). Some examples: the Department of Labor administers the Fair Labor Standards Act of 1938, which sets a minimum wage and time-and-a-half pay for over 40 hours a week for nonsupervisory employees. The Labor Department shares with the Internal Revenue Service oversight of the Employee Retirement Income Security Act of 1970. The Occupational Safety and Health Administration (OSHA), created in 1970, enforces safety standards. The Equal Employment Opportunity Commission administers the Americans with Disabilities Act of 1990, which requires employers to use all feasible means for employing persons with physical or mental impairments. The EEOC shares with the NLRB enforcement of Title VII of the Civil Rights Act of 1964, which bans employers and unions from discriminating on grounds of race, color, gender, and national origin.

and employer cannot agree on the appropriate members, the decision on the composition of the unit goes to the NLRB.

Elections are held to certify or decertify a union or to replace one with another. An election can be scheduled when 30 percent or more of the members of a bargaining unit have indicated that they want to vote. All full-time workers can vote: part-timers and workers on layoff or on strike are also eligible "if they have a reasonable expectation of continued employment or reemployment" (Gold, 1989, p. 30). If there is a dispute over the election, a union or employer must file an unfair labor practices charge with the NLRB, and a ruling is made after a hearing. If an organizing campaign is at issue, the board may issue a *bargaining order*, which requires an employer to recognize a union if the board determines that the employer's numerous and serious unfair labor practices have prevented a fair election. If either party to a ruling does not comply, the NLRB uses the courts to enforce its decisions. An NLRB ruling may be appealed in the federal courts, all the way to the Supreme Court.

Created by the Labor Act and drawing on this body of law, The National Labor Relations Board hears unfair labor practice cases, issues decisions and remedies, has responsibility for union certification and decertification elections, and administers parts of the Civil Rights Act of 1964 that apply to unions and employers. The NLRB is thus given a main role in America's system of industrial relations.

The Growth and Decline of Unions

In 1778, journeyman printers in New York City formed a union, demanded a wage increase, and received it (U.S. Department of Labor, 1979), and in 1886 a number of craft unions created the forerunner of the present American Federation of Labor. Although unions thus have been around for a long time, shaky legal grounds for a time restricted their growth. The road to organizing was cleared by the changed political and economic climate of the Great Depression of the 1930s, which led to enactment of the Wagner Act.

Since the 1930s, Table 4–1 shows, organized labor's share of the nonagricultural labor force first increased and then slumped. The plateau was reached in the mid-1940s, when 36 percent of employees saw unions as offering advantages and joined. The percentage of organized workers soon changed direction, however, and has since eroded.

The bottom part of Table 4–1 indicates union membership by certain variables, including the public and private sectors and the most heavily organized industries in the private sector. Yet between 1983 and 1994, union membership in manufacturing plunged nearly 70 percent, and

Table 4–1
Union Membership as a Percent of the Nonagricultural Labor Force,
United States, 1930–1993

Year	Union Membership
1930	12%
1935	13
1940	27
1945	36
1950	32
1955	33
1960	31
1965	30
1970	28
1975	27
1980	25
1985	18
1990	16
1993	16
1993 union members as a percent of:	
Male employees	18%
Female employees	13
Full-time workers	18
Part-time workers	7
Workers in:	
Government (public sector)	38
Private sector	11
Transport and utilities	31
Construction	20
Manufacturing	19

Sources: U.S. Department of Labor, Bureau of Labor Statistics, *Handbook of Labor Statistics 1975*, Reference Edition (Washington, DC), p. 389, and *News*, September 18, 1981; February 6, 1991; February 9, 1994; U.S. Bureau of the Census, *Statistical Abstract of the United States: 1987*, p. 409.

about one out of four members was lost in construction and transportation and public utilities. In those same years, unions gained in the public sector, but only by 3 percent (*Statistical Abstract*, 1994, p. 439).

The data in Table 4–1 include white-collar *employee associations*, such as the American Federation of Teachers, Airline Pilots Association, American Nurses Association, and the Federation of Physicians and Dentists. Members of these groups, therefore, are counted as unionists. As the proportion of blue-collar workers has declined, without the entry of professional, technical, and other white-collar employees to the ranks of organized labor, the proportions of unionized employees would inevitably be even smaller. Unionization (or equivalent associations) has had marked success among professionals and near-professionals in the public sector—teachers, social workers, postal workers, firefighters,

Table 4–2
Unionization Rates in Industrialized Countries, 1992/1993

Country	Union Members, Percent of Labor Force
United Kingdom	32%
Germany (West)	40
France	10
Netherlands	25
Belgium	77
Italy	15
Switzerland	29
Sweden	84
Norway	63
Denmark	80
Canada	30
Japan	24
Israel	56
Australia	40
United States	16

Sources: U.S. Department of Labor, Bureau of International Affairs, Foreign Labor Trends, 1993–1994, individual reports by country (Washington, DC, 1994, 1995).

police officers. In the private sector, professionals and other white-collar employees have been less willing to join unions.

Increased employment in the public sector, accompanied by state laws that permit collective bargaining, provided conditions in the 1960s and 1970s that favored organizing efforts. Toward the end of those years, however, public-sector growth lost momentum. Barbash (1980, p. 574) notes that "Public-sector bargaining represents a collective-bargaining breakthrough which is, for its time, comparable in historical importance to the first collective bargaining 'revolution' of the 1930s. But public-sector expansion and its union population seem to be slowing down earlier than did the private sector in an analogous stage." The small gains by public-sector unions in recent years have been overwhelmed by large losses in the private sector.

For comparison, unionization rates in a number of other industrialized countries are shown in Table 4–2. The Scandinavian countries—Sweden, Norway, Denmark—have relatively high unionization rates, whereas the United States, France, and Italy are on the low end. While the share of American unions in the labor force has decreased since the 1950s, worker organizations in Western Europe grew until the 1980s, when losses began to mount. In Japan, unions started to lose ground in the mid-1970s, and, as in Europe, the decline has persisted. Most industrialized countries now have a lower union density (organized workers' share of the labor force) than they had earlier (Freeman, 1994).

Collective Bargaining

When union density falls, U.S. workers are more broadly affected than those in Europe, due to differences in union-government ties, the scope of legislation, and forms of negotiating. Labor unions in Western Europe are linked to political parties; each benefits from the other's support. These relationships, and historical concern with preempting communist platforms, have encouraged the passage of national laws to regulate numerous workplace issues.

Many European governments require that corporate boards of directors include workers' representatives as voting members, and they may mandate *works councils* in which employees discuss operational and broader issues and recommend actions (Adams, 1995). Moreover, European governments have mandated such employee benefits as health insurance plans, annual vacations, sick leave with substantial pay, maternity leave with pay, and severance pay (Freeman, 1994). American employers may voluntarily offer such benefits, but smaller firms, especially, are inclined to provide few. Since most workplace issues are left to unions and employers, as unions decline, workers' collective concerns are less likely to be heard by employers or government in the United States.

European unions at the local level are relatively distant from pay issues. Employers' federations and union coalitions negotiate wages and working conditions for an entire sector, industry, or country, and regardless of workplace size, employers are held to the settlement. Freeman (1994, p. 16) notes: "The social partners are the main union federations and main employer groups. They conduct most collective negotiations, and European governments typically consult them on economic matters and often seek their consent on policies relating to wage inflation, job-creating initiatives, training programs, and the like." This is why there is less wage inequality in Europe. Negotiated agreements have raised lower-skilled workers' wages higher than market forces alone would have. On the negative side, however, this has contributed to notably skimpy job creation.

In contrast to the involvement of European unions with political parties, American labor unions have focused mainly on bargainable, bread-and-butter issues, while remaining wary of broad economic theories and political alliances (Barkin, 1991). This practical approach began with Samuel Gompers' leadership of the newly formed American Federation of Labor. As Gompers (1919) put it:

> The primary essential in our mission has been the protection of the wage-worker, now; to increase his wages; to cut hours off the long workday,...to improve the safety and the sanitary conditions of the work-shop.... These, in the nature of things, I repeat, were and are the primary objects of trade unionism. (p. 8)

In the United States, collective bargaining is basically an adversary relationship. Each side of the negotiations—with labor representatives literally on one side of a table and management on the other—initially demands more than it really expects to receive, while the other side offers less than it will finally give. If the negotiations do not produce a satisfactory outcome, the talks may break off and result in a strike or lockout (management temporarily closes down a business to put economic pressure on the employees). If the negotiations are successful, the union's members must still approve the proposed contract.

The contract negotiation process ordinarily concludes with a settlement. Strikes actually account for only a slight loss of work time. The highest rate was in 1946, when over 1 percent of total work hours were lost to strikes; in the 1990s, work time lost to strikes is a tiny fraction of 1 percent (*Statistical Abstract*, 1994, p. 438; U.S. Department of Labor, 1975a, p. 390). The threat of resorting to a strike or lockout encourages the bargainers to compromise their demands and reach a settlement. Public employees are prohibited from striking by most states, and strikes in essential services (fire, police) are barred by nearly every state. This has not always stopped public-sector employees, particularly teachers, from threatening to strike and sometimes doing so.[7] In the end, bargaining is a power relationship, and the terms of the agreement reflect that fact.

The representatives of labor and management are required by the Labor Act to "bargain in good faith"—they must attempt to reach agreement. But the obligation to bargain does not demand that either party accept a proposal or make concessions. The employer is required to provide information relevant to bargaining, such as fringe benefit costs and job classifications. If labor accuses management of withholding relevant data, or either side accuses the other of not bargaining in good faith, the dispute goes to the NLRB.

When union and management representatives negotiate a contract, the Labor Act specifies that wages, hours, and conditions of employment are mandatory topics that must be included because they directly affect the employment relationship. The primary mandatory issues (Gold, 1989, p. 41) are pay rate, method of pay (hourly, salary, piece rate), hours of work, work rules, safety, promotions, health insurance, pensions, order of layoffs, benefits for laid-off workers, discipline policies, and grievance and arbitration procedures. Other topics, such as policies that favor gender or race discrimination, are illegal. If a topic is

---

[7]In addition to legal remedies, there are other restraints on public-sector disputes. As in the private sector, strikers lose their wages. But in contrast to the for-profit sector, replacement workers are rarely hired by governments, so officials are pressured to settle if public services are disrupted (transportation, schools, sewage, fire, police, and so on).

Figure 4–1
Some Clauses of a Union-Management Contract

Article XI: Strikes and Lockouts

11.1   The union shall not engage in, authorize, sanction or condone its members taking part in, nor shall any of its members engage in or take part in any strike, including sympathy strikes, picketing or work stoppage involving the Company's operations, premises or equipment during the term of this Agreement or any extension thereof, as long as the Union and/or the members do not engage in or take part in any strike, picketing or work stoppages involving the Company's operations, premises or equipment, the Company agrees that there shall be no lockout during the term of this Agreement or any extensions thereof.

Article XII: Service Contracts

12.1   As a matter of stated policy, the Company will not permanently lay off regular employees from their regular line of work in order to contract out that work, provided that, this policy is not to be construed as limiting the full right of management to contract out work for any other reason or purpose.

Article XIII: Check-Off

13.1   Upon receipt of a properly executed written authorization from an employee who is covered by this Agreement, the Company agrees, until notified otherwise by the employee, to deduct the regular dues of the Union from the pay of the employee once per month and to remit such deduction to the Financial Secretary of Local 1700 within ten (10) days from the date of the deduction. The Company shall be notified in writing by the Financial Secretary of Local 1700 of any change in the regular dues structure by the fifteenth (15th) day of the month in which the change shall be effective.

Article XIX: Hours of Work and Overtime

19.1   Employees shall work on a scheduled basis under which the regular work day shall not exceed eight (8) hours and the regular work week shall not exceed forty (40) hours. Work in excess of eight (8) hours in any one day shall be at the overtime rate. In cases of emergency or when deemed expedient by the Company, employees may be required to work more than the number of hours specified above.

19.2   All time worked in excess of the regular hours on a day when an employee is regularly on duty and all time worked on a day when an employee is regularly off duty shall be considered as overtime.

19.3   The overtime rate of pay shall be one and one-half (1½) times the regular base rate for the particular employee's classification. The overtime rate shall be used for overtime work as specified above.

Source: Contract between Transit Management of Southeast Louisiana Inc. and the International Brotherhood of Electrical Workers, for the period July 1986 to June 1989.

neither mandated nor unlawful, it is permissible provided both sides agree to negotiate it. An example is employee discounts for an employer's product.

Figure 4–1 reproduces several clauses from a union-management contract. Notice the detailed, legalistic style. This contract was relatively short; some run to hundreds of pages. All are complex documents, and opinions can differ on their meaning. Resolving these disagreements involves arbitration under the rules of the National Labor Relations Board.

The American system of settling disputes is built on contracts that call for mediation or, most often, arbitration (Gould, 1993, ch. 8). *Mediation* involves a third party who makes proposals for resolving an impasse. The proposals are not binding, so the mediator must attempt to persuade the parties to accept them. Unions and employers can select mutually acceptable mediators from individuals listed by the Federal Mediation and Conciliation Service or the American Arbitration Association. *Fact-finding* is a related process. The fact finder is a neutral third party who looks into the facts of the disputed issues and makes non-binding recommendations. Current contracts require mediation (and fact-finding) less frequently than in the past, largely because they are not binding. Both management and labor worry that if voluntary methods fail to resolve a dispute, customers might be permanently lost if the business were disrupted by strike or lockout.

Arbitration, however, is binding, and it is very widely used. Contracts ordinarily list the steps. First, before resorting to an arbitrator, the foreman and shop steward (a worker delegated by the union to handle grievances) must attempt to resolve the problem immediately. If the complaint remains unsettled, the next step is a union-management committee. The grievance may be pushed upward several times to committees of increasingly higher-level union and management officials. If the grievance remains unresolved, a third party is jointly selected to rule on the dispute. After each side has presented its case, the arbitrator's interpretation of the contract determines whose claim is valid.

In some cases, the union may believe that both the contract and the Labor Act have been violated when an unfair labor practice is involved (for instance, the union steward is fired for encouraging grievances). The union can request arbitration for violation of the contract or appeal to the NLRB to remedy the unfair labor practice. The NLRB, however, usually requires arbitration as a first step. If the union wins, the contract was misinterpreted by management, and an unfair labor practice charge can be filed. But when arbitration finds that the management interpretation was correct, then management cannot be accused of an unfair labor practice.

If a contract includes arbitration of grievances and the employer refuses, the union can ask a federal court to order the employer to accept arbitration. Sometimes a union might opt not to arbitrate and instead go on strike. If the friction is over an arbitratable issue (according to the contract), the employer could request the court for an injunction against the strike and an order requiring the union to arbitrate. In short, arbitration is the preferred remedy for disputes under the Labor Act and by the federal courts.

These methods for handling disagreements are unlike those in Europe; European unions are usually not involved with local grievances. Employees at the company level are represented by works councils that typically deal with these matters, while unions focus on collective bargaining at the national or regional level (Rogers and Streeck, 1994).

Grievance arbitration has been quite successful in resolving labor-management disputes. Walkouts or shutouts have been largely avoided, but achieving a contract, especially at the organizing stage, has proven far stormier. Each year, most of the thousands of cases of unfair labor practices charges brought to the NLRB involve discipline or discharge of workers for prounion activities during organizing campaigns (Gould, 1993). Illegal tactics by employers range from intimidating workers who are sympathetic to unions, to using job interviews to screen out union-friendly applicants (Robinson and McIlwee, 1989; Saltzman, 1994). This situation is reflected in the data on union density.

Prospects for Labor Organizations

Partly for historical reasons, employers in the United States are inclined to avoid unions, as we have noted. In contrast to the more centralized European pattern, the American system largely decentralizes the determination of employees' wages and benefits to the enterprise level. Unionization thus raises the stakes for employers. Moreover, if an employer uses unlawful tactics to derail an organizing drive, the legal remedies are neither severe not timely. Additionally, competitive economic pressures have sharply increased attention to labor costs. As many American employers see it, the structure of incentives does not favor worker organizations (Chaison and Rose, 1991). Neither does the long-term shift of employment out of manufacturing, which has depleted the unions' traditional industrial base.

In general, currently unionized employees do profit from their membership. But by how much? A possible complication is that compensation in unionized firms has affected nonunion firms. Employers may follow wage guidelines, at least roughly, in order to avoid a union. That sort of ripple effect has dwindled, however, accompanying the drop in unionization of workplaces. But there still are substantial pay differences between unionized workers and others. In the early 1990s, private-sector and public-sector employees represented by unions had about a 20 percent wage edge over nonunion workers. Among people doing approximately similar work, wage gains from collective bargaining ranged from none (finance, insurance, real estate) to over 50 percent (construction). Unionized manufacturing workers, for example, had a 13 percent advantage; for workers in services, it was 15 percent (*Statistical Abstract*, 1994, p. 439). Benefits, too, are better among unionized employees ("Why America Needs Unions," 1994). Under pressure from lower-wage, nonunion shops across town (not to mention offshore), however, organized labor's compensation advantage can only erode. It has been estimated that every year more than 300,000 new members would have to join American unions just to keep even in the private sector. That many new members is several times the number added annually by NLRB elections (Chaison and Dhavale, 1990).

To reverse the unions' slide, observers have proposed various strategies. These include establishing closer ties with a major political party; lobbying for federally mandated works councils and reform of union recognition laws; negotiating for placement of union delegates on corporate boards of directors; cooperating with worker participation programs; or applying more organizing efforts to service industries and less to manufacturing (Turner, 1994; Kochan and Wever, 1991). Political party affiliation and nationally mandated works councils, ideas borrowed from Europe, probably reach beyond what is feasible in the United States. On the other hand, during times of national crisis, unions and employers have supported labor-management committees within firms. Unions could publicly endorse programs of employee problem-solving and quality improvement. Though this would be unlikely to dramatically turn their losses around, some unionized plants have had notable success with such plans. The Saturn Division of General Motors, which builds the Saturn car, and New United Motors Manufacturing, a G.M.–Toyota joint venture that makes the Geo Prism and Corolla, are frequently cited as examples (Charles and Bennett, 1993; Boyett and Conn, 1992). There is a hitch, however.

Because the Labor Act envisioned an arm's-length relationship, it impedes labor-management cooperation in nonunionized and unionized enterprises. Although the NLRB and the federal courts have tended not to interfere in employee-involvement programs, there are also contrary decisions; no clear guidelines have emerged (Hogler and Grenier, 1992, ch. 3). The problem centers on the prohibition of management domination of a labor organization. According to Section 2(5) of the Wagner Act, a labor organization is "any organization of any kind, or any agency or employee representation committee or plan, in which employees participate and which exists for the purpose, in whole or in part, of dealing with employers concerning grievances, labor disputes, wages, rates of pay, hours of employment, or conditions of work."

Any labor-management committee, works council, quality circle, or other sort of employee-involvement group could be considered a labor organization if the discussion just touched on wages, hours, or working conditions. The same group might be viewed as management dominated because it is company sponsored, meets on paid company time, and all or some worker-members were selected by management. Until the law is changed, the NLRB or the courts could decide against most existing employee-participation programs.

SUMMARY

Achievement, rather than ascription, is emphasized in industrial societies. Still, the family origins of workers continue to be important, largely because of the material and cultural advantages or disadvantages that affect children's schooling. Educational credentials are the single most important factor in reaching a higher socioeconomic status through occupational mobility.

Women's and men's intergenerational mobility alike tilts upward; however, there is a smaller payoff for women because they less often enter the highly rewarded occupations. Opportunities for getting ahead hinge on the supply of attractive jobs. The evidence suggests that upward movement in both worklife and between-generations mobility began to slow in the 1980s.

Collective bargaining in the United States was made lawful by the Wagner Act in the midst of the Great Depression. Nonsupervisory employees have the right to organize, and employers are required to recognize certified unions and negotiate with their representatives. In the 1950s, over 30 percent of the labor force was in unions, but union membership had dropped to about 15 percent by the 1990s. Some observers have suggested that union cooperation in worker-involvement programs may be an important step toward restoring organizing momentum. To give employee participation a clear legal footing, however, labor law will need to be reformed.

5 Overview: Looking Back and Ahead

RETROSPECT

With the collapse of the Roman Empire in the fifth century, the areas of the Western world formerly under Roman rule slipped into anarchy. No central administration or regional governments existed to stop the bandits who roamed the deteriorating highways or the pirates who controlled the Mediterranean Sea. Transporting goods was a dangerous venture attempted by increasingly fewer traders. From these conditions emerged the self-reliant manor, ruled by its lord and producing its own goods. After this type of self-contained production began to slacken in the eleventh century, manorial goods were supplemented by the craft guilds' products and merchant guilds' imports. Merchandise was becoming increasingly available in the growing medieval towns, but the land remained the source of livelihood for all but the relatively few town dwellers. As late as the 1700s, nine out of ten people everywhere lived by farming. Although the putting-out system gradually displaced guilds, cottage industry was always only a meager supplement to the agricultural incomes of rural families.

The rise of the factory system—first in Britain, and then spreading to Western Europe and the United States—transformed the source of earnings among the millions of people drawn into towns to find work. Within the brief span of a hundred years, the industrialized Western nations were dotted with large urban centers of manufacturing, commerce, and finance. In the United States the pace of industrialization was compressed into a remarkably few decades. Spurred in the 1860s by the Civil War's enormous appetite for manufactured goods, American industry made up for lost time. By the 1890s, U.S. industrial output equaled that of England, France, and Germany combined.

Along with industrialization, standards of living improved. The abrupt increase of material goods is well described by Daniel Bell (1975):

> From the earliest times, back to two thousand years before Christ, down to the eighteenth century, there was no very great change in the standard of life of the average man in the civilized centres of earth. But with the combination of technical efficiency and capital accumulation, mankind had discovered the "magic" of "compound interest," of growth building on growth.... Think of this in terms of material things—houses, transport and the like. (pp. 459–60)

Despite depressions and recessions, even the nearly total wartime destruction of manufacturing capacity, the industrialized nations—with the notable exception of former Soviet-bloc countries—have delivered a rising standard of consumption to most citizens. Certainly the average American family's living standards have improved over the years, with an exceptionally rapid and sizable gain between the end of World War II and the mid-1970s. From then to now, however, average real earnings have been flat.

The Good Times, 1950–1975, and After

With the end of conflict in Europe and Asia, the next few decades turned out to be the best of times for many Americans. In 1945, America's enemies had unconditionally surrendered. Their cities were in ruins and factories largely rubble. The former allies in Europe were only marginally less devastated. Their treasuries had been drained and manufacturing plants damaged or destroyed. Left standing was the immense production capacity of the United States, its infrastructure, factories, and labor force. As the economist Lester Thurow (1992, p. 246) describes the situation: "America's economic dominance after World War II (it had over half of the world's GNP and was the technological leader in essentially every industrial product) had not been seen since the Roman Empire and probably will not again be seen in the next two thousand years."

Half the world's gross national production! And Americans benefited with jobs and income. During those postwar years, unemployment was relatively low, poverty rates dropped by 40 to 50 percent among both black and white families, and the average family's real purchasing power almost doubled. Nevertheless, America's dominant position in world output had started to wane.

The U.S. share of world production slipped to about 30 percent in the 1960s, then dropped to 20 percent in the 1980s. In comparison,

Japan's portion of global GNP, which accounted for only 2 percent in the 1950s, grew fivefold by 1980, and Western Europe's share caught up with America's in the mid-1970s (Okita, 1985). Other signs of trouble ahead were also visible. While Americans' incomes were rising, the federal budget ran 16 annual deficits between 1946 and 1968. The budget was balanced in 1969, but that was the last time.

The nation's debt steadily climbed. Interest on the national debt in 1969 was about 7 percent of federal outlays, and it doubled by 1994 (*Statistical Abstract*, 1994, p. 332). Mounting debt-interest costs, along with the large entitlement programs of Social Security, Medicare, and Medicaid, now restrain "discretionary" spending. Plans for starting new programs or upgrading current ones are difficult to sell.

Consider, too, that the standard plan for recovery from recession is financial stimulation. Reducing interest rates should encourage business investment and personal consumption, and spending federal funds should increase jobs—repair and construction of schools, roads and bridges, and public transportation systems. In 1993, when President Clinton's administration faced a recession, the Federal Reserve Board quickly reduced interest rates. But when Clinton asked for new spending, Congress refused, although the president and a majority of the Congress were Democrats. Because of chronic overspending when the economic climate was comfortable, additional borrowing when the economy had slowed was an unattractive option. With sizable annual deficits projected from 1995 to the year 2000, the national debt likely will be approaching $1 trillion above the current $5 trillion. Economically and politically, it is increasingly painful to respond to economic downturns, or social problems, with more debt expansion.

In the early 1970s, the budget deficit was joined by another unwelcome development. For the first time since World War II, America's balance of trade tipped from favorable to unfavorable—imported goods cost more than the dollars brought in by exports. The trade imbalance then expanded.[1] Even though a persistent surplus in services—banking, insurance, consulting, legal services, transportation, tourism, royalties, license fees, and others—offset the unfavorable trade position, this surplus eventually fell behind the growing trade imbalance in goods. By 1982 the *current account* (the combined value of goods and services) was in deficit, and it has remained so. In the 1980s, by comparison, Japan and Germany had trade surpluses. The value of Japan's

---

[1]With no federal debt, there would be a smaller trade deficit. If the government's outlays were supported without borrowing, taxes would have to rise to maintain the spending. Government borrowing thus allows taxpayers to retain more income which can be used to buy goods, including imports. This convenient arrangement is flawed in the long run.

exports nearly matched America's, and West Germany's surpassed it ("New Export Champs," 1986). Thurow (1992) estimates that America loses over 2.5 million full-time jobs with each $100 billion shortfall in trade. In the mid-1990s, the overall trade imbalance for the United States exceeded $100 billion. The origins of this situation can be found in the Cold War with the Soviet bloc.

From Dominant to One among Equals

America's world-trade recovery strategy performed brilliantly in the postwar years. In 1944, two international financial agencies, the International Monetary Fund (IMF) and the International Bank for Reconstruction and Development (the World Bank), were established at a global conference in Bretton Woods, New Hampshire. The IMF, designed to facilitate trade by stabilizing international monetary exchange rates, proved effective. In part this was because most of the postwar trade was priced in dollars, and the dollar was a steady, gold-backed currency.[2] The World Bank's task originally was to finance rebuilding in countries devastated by war. Before long it was providing grants or loans to less-developed countries for projects such as electricity generation, pipelines, and airports.

The General Agreement on Tariffs and Trade (GATT), sponsored by the United States, was signed in 1947 by the world's industrialized nations. While equal tariffs was not the goal, tariffs were lowered and their use restricted.[3] To further speed the recovery of war-damaged nations, the Marshall Plan was conceived in 1948, providing billions of dollars to Western Europe. Altogether, between 1950 and 1960, the U.S. foreign aid bill was $50 billion, a huge amount at the time (*World Almanac*, 1995).

America had generously assisted friends and foes alike to rebuild their infrastructures and industries, and it had also offered access to its home market. By the mid-1950s Western Europe's economies had more than recovered to prewar levels, and Japan's citizens were on the road to parity with Western living standards. Moreover, in South Korea, Taiwan, and other Asian countries, industrial development was progressing and living standards were rising.

---

[2]The United States partly left the gold standard in 1933, making dollars held by individuals no longer convertible to a fixed amount of gold stored by the federal government. This allows the Federal Reserve Board to manage the money supply more easily; by adjusting interest rates, and thereby credit expansion, the economy can be slowed or stimulated. However, with too much credit growth, inflation may result, and with too little, there may be a recession.

[3]There was, however, no institutional means of enforcing the GATT trade rules. The American negotiators had rejected the creation of an international body to administer the policies. In the 1994 GATT, they approved an international mechanism to settle trade disputes among the economic competitors.

America's post-1945 policies were largely a response to the Cold War. In this global contest, the United States and the U.S.S.R. each attempted to win converts to its political and economic system, or at least to block the other's advance. Democratic capitalism confronted the command economy of the centralized state. To prevent the spread of communist or procommunist regimes, economic links were formed between the United States and certain nations. Thus foreign aid to alleviate misery was both ethically desirable and politically useful.

Trade also created ties. Foreign aid helped to reconstruct damaged factories, and the United States provided a market so earnings from exports of the products made in weaker economies would provide capital for further investment and eventual prosperity. It worked. The U.S. market was opened without demanding reciprocity from West Europe, Japan, and other countries that protected their own growing industrial bases.

In the context of the Cold War, a willingness to import goods from reviving industries made sense, especially if the imported products were no threat to American industries. They were technologically far ahead of others, making products, such as the Boeing 707, that could not be made overseas. Thurow (1992) explains other advantages:

> ...in 1950 the American market was more than nine times as large as the next largest market.... American industry enjoyed economies of scale...that no other national economy could hope to achieve. Mass manufacturing was effectively an American monopoly, where unit costs in industries such as autos or steel were beyond the dreams of the largest foreign producers. Serving such a large internal market, specialty firms could thrive. (p. 154)

As we now know, the weak economies strengthened, America's markets remained open, and reciprocity is still uneven. With the breakdown of the Soviet Union the justification for U.S. trade policies has shifted. It is assumed that all nations and their populations gain by removing trade barriers—the benefits of competition have become the dominant theme. But competition does not everywhere have the same meaning.

Industrial Structures

Few would currently defend the notion that economic growth is served by the absence of competition. The dismal performance of command economies is a fact. Consumer goods in the Soviet Union and mainland China, for example, were chronically in short supply. (In contrast, capitalist economies suffer from the reverse problem—supply periodically exceeds demand, with the familiar cycle of rising and falling unemployment.) Command economies are just that: What will be produced, where, prices of goods and services, and wages are among the endless administrative decisions made by governments.

Command Economies and Free Markets

The underlying idea of command economies was that centrally planned production would be more efficient than market systems with their competing producers. Actual results turned out quite the opposite. One main problem was the extravagant number of personnel on payrolls. Observers of command economies have offered different explanations: "Employment is not primarily a market relationship....Employment plays a welfare role: it is a value in itself" (Walder, 1986, p. 11). "Once factories...were granted budgetary lines for a certain number of employees, they were automatically allocated the money to pay the salaries.... As a result...administrators had strong incentive to increase the labor force and none to reduce it" (Lehmann, 1995, p. 206). The relationship between the state and its enterprises in command economies is summarized by Stark and Nee (1989, p. 10): "The paternalism...in public ownership guarantees the firm's survival by the state regardless of its performance.... Because budget constraints are lax, the firm has little pressure to use resources and investments efficiently."

Full employment was an ideological priority, whereas efficiency was not. Enterprises could operate within these guidelines because money-losing companies were kept afloat with subsidies. The last Soviet president, Mikhail Gorbachev, attempted to restructure the economy in the late 1980s by eliminating these costly subsidies, thus allowing firms to go bankrupt and, of course, job protection to be eliminated. At about the same time, mainland China's leaders attempted to break "the iron rice bowl"—once employed, a job was for life. In both instances, there were public and Communist Party objections to the reforms. It was anticipated that if subsidies to state enterprises ended, large-scale unemployment would trigger political turmoil. Implementation was delayed, and it remains incomplete.

Russia still props up many money-losing state enterprises, and agriculture continues to depend on the inefficient Soviet-style collective farms. However, about half the state's enterprises have been sold. While China avoided the upheaval that hastened privatization in Russia, it, too, subsidizes state enterprises. Its private sector, however, is expanding at an extraordinary clip. Moreover, China has the great advantage of an effective agricultural base. After the communal form of agriculture was shifted to the "responsibility system" of family farming in the 1970s, agricultural productivity climbed (Tausky, 1991). Russia and mainland China are headed toward more competitive markets.

The classic command economy and American-style capitalism, however, do not exhaust the alternatives. There are varieties of the free-market system in Europe and Asia that differ from the U.S. pattern in several ways that follow from their limited faith in the benefits of unrestrained free markets:

1. Protection of domestic industries is more widely practiced through tariffs and other import restrictions.
2. Business is often organized in a manner that is illegal in the United States: firms are interlocked, and banks may be included.
3. Government and business are less at loggerheads: more cooperation and more subsidies result.

Japan and mainland China shelter their home industries with a modern version of mercantilism. Despite large trade surpluses with the United States, China restricts foreign participation in basic sectors such as cars, power generation, and telecommunications ("Eyeball to Eyeball," 1995). Japan runs a trade surplus with every nation; while its official tariffs are low, a web of business ties and customs regulations limits imports to a much smaller share of the market than among other industrialized countries (Holstein, 1994). Newly developing East Asian nations, such as South Korea, Singapore, and Malaysia, have noted Japan's impressive success with protectionist, export-led development and are following that model.

Business Groups

The *keiretsu* or business groups of Japan are organized around cross-shareholding, interlocked corporate boards, joint projects, and information exchange, sometimes with a bank as the financial center of the cluster. The hundreds of companies in each of the half dozen major *keiretsu* comprise a semiclosed grouping (Harrison, 1994, ch. 7). Together, the *keiretus* control stock equal to over half the total value of the shares traded on the Tokyo Stock Exchange. Opening Japanese companies' doors to U.S. products requires more than good prices and quality. For instance, Fuji Heavy Industries assembles Subaru cars, and the *keiretsu* members produce the components. Moreover, the producers of Subarus, Toyotas, and other makes of automobiles also own many of the dealerships (Womack, Jones, and Roos, 1990).

Not only are Japanese business structures organized differently than those in the United States, so are most others. For example, Germany's business groups, while more loosely assembled than the *keiretsu*, are centered on banks. The Deutsche Bank holds a substantial share of

Daimler-Benz and dozens of other companies. Germany's other major banks and large firms are similarly linked. Industry in South Korea, Taiwan, Malaysia, Indonesia, and Thailand is built around networks of family-owned enterprises ("The Triple Revolution," 1994). *Keiretsu* or comparable arrangements are arguably illegal under American antitrust law, and U.S. critics have recommended antitrust suits against *keiretsu* operating in this country, charging that they systematically exclude American companies as suppliers.

Also clearly illegal in U.S. law is bank ownership of stock in other businesses, a uniquely American prohibition enacted in the Glass-Steagall Act of 1933. The legislation was designed to stop banks from speculating in securities; it also prevents the creation of U.S. business group relationships that include a bank. Some analysts now urge overturning Glass-Steagall, arguing that business groups have advantages, and, since these arrangements are allowed elsewhere, for competitive reasons they should be permitted here (Thurow, 1992). This argument is worth considering. A business group with cross-shareholding has oversight of member firms through interlocked boards of directors. If Kodak, Sears, IBM, or GM, for instance, had been monitored in the 1980s by detail-minded directors who could demand preventive actions, the extensive layoffs and plunging market shares of these firms might have been averted.

Mutual oversight can forestall, too, the poison pills, greenmail, and golden parachutes that benefit no one except top managers.[4] Cross-shareholding also provides shelter for longer-term and larger investments in training and research and development, because there is less pressure for constantly growing profits. A slackening of growth may prompt impatient shareholders to sell a laggard's stock, pulling down its value.[5] The impact of outsiders' sales, however, can be muted by substantial cross-shareholding within a business group. Such groups also can provide the best possible technical and marketing advice to member firms, since it is in everyone's economic interest to do so, and with a bank in the group, the financing of promising though risky projects is surer.

The Role of Government

The view that government should emphasize regulation instead of assistance is also not shared around the globe. To illustrate: South Korea provides easily available, subsidized low-interest loans for developing

---

[4]A poison pill is a large debt taken on as a takeover defense. Golden parachutes are oversize severance packages for executives. Greenmail offers above-market prices for stock in order to prevent a takeover attempt. Executives use the firm's resources for this costly defensive maneuver.

[5]Pension and mutual funds are major stockholders, and their managers are often intolerant of slow earnings growth. It is not unusual for a fund to annually turn over half or more of its holdings.

technically advanced exports. Samsung (one of the world's 10 largest, fastest-growing computer chip makers) and other Korean firms are designing semiconductors for high-end products with huge markets in cellular phones, digital VCRs, and programmable microwave ovens (Markoff, 1995). When the Japanese government defined the recession of the 1960s as deepened by "excessive competition," it was led to take such actions as "organizing antirecession cartels and vigorous export campaigns, erecting barriers to foreign direct investment, and structuring the financial system to favor industrial investments (especially in targeted industries) over consumption" (U.S. Congress, 1991, p. 7). Japan's Ministry of International Trade and Industry (MITI) assists export-oriented firms. It scouts markets, arranges loans, and subsidizes and organizes research on cutting-edge technologies, especially those with spillover effects on the rest of the economy, such as memory chips. MITI has encouraged protection of key industries—steel, autos, chemicals, and electronic equipment. Aside from agricultural products (rice, apples), trade barriers persist in the 1990s (Neff, 1995).

In Europe, a sizable number of commercial enterprises in autos, steel, banks, and chemicals are wholly or partly government owned, especially in France, Germany, and Italy. State-run power generation and distribution, and telephone and telegraph service, are the rule among most members of the 15-country European Union (EU).[6] The EU governments also organize and subsidize dozens of massive research programs in such strategic sectors as communications, information technology, and energy. A variant on this is the direct sponsorship of a start-up competitive industry. In order to enter the passenger-airplane production business and break Boeing's dominance, several West Europe governments jointly provided the enormous funds needed to design and build the Airbus. State-owned airlines then provided a ready market. In 1990, with the Boeing 747 excluded (Airbus has no equivalent plane), Boeing's global market share of new orders dipped below that of Airbus (Thurow, 1992). Likewise, railcar production is thriving in Europe, boosted by state-aided credit for transit systems that purchase them. America's last producer of passenger railcars is on the way to exiting the business (Sterngold, 1995). With the exception of the United States, Canada, Britain, and Australia, all of which favor laissez-faire economics, an industrial strategy is a component of national policy in nearly every country ("Triple Revolution," 1994).

---

[6]Financial help is common for enterprises in which governments have invested , some of which compete with independent companies at home and elsewhere. The EU has scheduled privatization for government-owned telephone companies in the late 1990s and broad deregulation of communications services.

Competition and capitalism thus have different meanings for America's trading partners. The United States, nevertheless, cannot control other countries' business structures or trade practices. The European Union, Japan, and China are equally able to write the rules of the game. Most of the EU countries have adopted standardized quality assurance criteria (called "ISO 9000 standards"). To produce in or export to the EU, manufacturers must have certification and periodic recertification by qualified examiners for their product designs, processes, and suppliers ("It's a Small Business World," 1995). American companies that want to do business in the European Union must follow its rules.

While the labels *free market* or *market economy* are handy, they do not actually describe the U.S. or any other industrialized economy. The roles of government in "capitalist" economies differ by degree. The United States, too, has some tariffs, though they typically are small (about 5 percent), import quotas (on clothing, textiles, peanuts, and sugar), restrictions (on exporting products with military uses), and subsidies (for farm products), to cite a few examples. The National Labor Relations Act and its administrative arm, the National Labor Relations Board, significantly affect labor relations. The U.S. Labor Department and the Environmental Protection Agency, Securities and Exchange Commission, Federal Trade Commission, Food and Drug Administration, and numerous other federal agencies influence the way business is done. The Federal Reserve Board is highly intrusive with its influence on interest rates. Moreover, these administrative interventions are joined by indispensable laws of contract, property rights, bankruptcy, and taxes. Although a free market is in reality impossible, America's way of doing business does give freer rein to market forces than most others do. This offers companies greater flexibility, while creating more insecurity for employees, whose jobs and benefits are always at risk.

The United States is a military superpower, yet the foremost challenge now is on the economic front. The competition is not only among firms, it is as much between the systems in which they are embedded. At stake is widening or narrowing Americans' access to a middle-class standard of living.

PROSPECTS

The High-Performance Workplace

Real incomes in the United States, on average, have stalled since the mid-1970s (see Chapter 3). Many analysts agree that for the nation to escape this dead end requires major changes in work site organization

(Hammer and Champy, 1993; Pinchot and Pinchot, 1993; Kochan and Osterman, 1994). The reasoning is this: Conventional workplaces are in hot competition for market share in this country and globally. Furthermore, there is worldwide excess capacity in many products and services, and somewhere labor is always cheaper. Together, these conditions limit market shares and constrain prices. To increase profits in this environment requires lower operating costs—materials, labor force, and so on. Taking cost-saving as the primary competitive strategy has been termed *the low-wage path*. The majority of U.S. firms are on that path (Appelbaum and Batt, 1994; Colclough and Tolbert, 1992).

This strategy, however, leaves basic problems untouched,[7] for a number of reasons:

1. Somewhere the product can be made at less cost by lower-wage employees. Therefore, expenses must be squeezed even harder.
2. Production processes are not reconfigured. After layoffs, employees who are left simply run the old processes with fewer hands.
3. Improving the quality of output is peripheral. If the product can pass final inspection, it is good enough for the market.
4. Enhancing organizational flexibility is neglected. The firm cannot respond in a timely manner to market shifts—the equipment is lacking, and workers are not technically trained to perform flexibly.
5. The organization is not designed to tap employees' participation in quality and productivity improvement.

The low-wage path is along the lines of Taylor's scientific management (see Chapters 2 and 3). Traditional Taylorist production methods were markedly successful in raising Americans' standards of living by providing cars, lawnmowers and dishwashers of "good enough" quality at reasonable cost. Strictly separated functions pervaded the companies that produced the goods—thinking was management's responsibility, while workers were responsible for performing easily learned tasks within an elaborate division of labor. In the first few decades after World War II, this arrangement delivered a steadily advancing standard of living. Cost-plus pricing allowed comfortable profits for the manufacturer and suppliers, and an acceptable share of the profits was passed on to workers. Relatively placid markets yielded agreeable results for companies and employees.

---

[7]Studies indicate that the results of change efforts focused mainly on scrimping are usually disappointing. Expected gains in productivity often do not materialize: instead, it slips lower (Cameron, Freeman, and Mishra, 1993).

When markets became turbulent, however, only a small fraction of companies responded by attempting a structural overhaul. Since this fraction depends on the analysts' methods, only rough estimates are possible. Clearly, more larger than smaller firms have adopted some or most of the methods described below; overall, they represent about one in five companies. Appelbaum and Batt (1993) conclude that from 10 to 25 percent of employees are in establishments that have substantially altered the organization of work. Whether producing goods or services, the high performance, high involvement, or transformed firms, as they are variously described, sharply diverge from the traditional bureaucratic pattern.

American versions of high performance developed by drawing on "best practices" from Germany, Japan, and elsewhere. While these are not uniform, high performers have several characteristics in common (Appelbaum and Batt, 1994; Heckscher and Donnellon, 1994; Boyett and Conn, 1992).[8] These characteristics include the following:

1. Structures are flatter. The traditional many-layered bureaucracy is cumbersome; decisions are too slow and too far from the relevant information. High-involvement firms *delayer*, removing layers, and push decisions down to the level nearest the problem.
2. The distinction between thinking and doing is blurred. Narrow tasks are replaced by broad team-based responsibilities, which include spotting and responding to in-process problems. Quality circles or other forms of teams meet periodically to analyze problems and offer ideas for improvement.
3. Extensive training is provided in team building and in task skills, including cross-training.
4. Information is broadly shared. Operational and financial data facilitate understanding of how the work unit and the company are performing relative to goals and competitors.
5. The organization attempts to maintain job security. This nurtures commitment and protects the firm's investment in training.
6. Performance pay is part of the compensation package. Effort is encouraged by profit sharing, gain sharing, and pay for knowledge.[9]

---

[8]Variations in emphasis have led to overlapping but distinguishable high-performance systems: "lean production" (Womack, Jones, and Roos, 1991) and "team production" (Wellins, Byham, and Wilson, 1991). The key difference is the extent of the workers' operational autonomy. In team production, the main source of operating decisions and improvement is the team, whereas lean production is a "parallel" system in which work groups, engineers, and managers are all involved.

[9]Profit sharing is based on companywide profitability. Gain sharing is tied to the work unit. If worker-controlled costs (such as fuel, scrap, labor time) are reduced relative to a standard cost, work-unit members share in the savings. Pay for knowledge is an individual pay increment for each skill in a set of competencies needed by a team. These pay systems can be used singly or combined.

7. Benchmarking is routinely used to measure current performance against the best competitors' quality, productivity, design time, customer satisfaction, and so on. Surpassing other firm's performance is the goal.

An example of how an American firm met the challenge of high performance is the experience of Motorola, which lost market share in the 1980s to Japanese companies with lower-priced, better-quality pagers, cellular phones, and semiconductors. By 1990, following sweeping changes, Motorola had matched or surpassed its competitors in these products (Boyett and Conn, 1992). Motorola cut layers of managers and supervisors, integrated departments to remove restraints on collaboration, and invested heavily in equipment and research and development. Employees were trained in job skills, problem solving, and quality assurance methods (statistical process control). Each group was made responsible for a segment of the process, including accuracy, timeliness, and cost improvement. A *total quality management* (TQM) approach was adopted to emphasize quality. (In TQM, the "customer" must be satisfied. Every work group is considered a provider to the next group down the line and a customer of the preceding group; thus customers are both internal and external to the organization.) Throughout Motorola, quality and productivity improvement teams were organized; these teams set goals and received bonuses for meeting them. Though job security was not an ironclad guarantee, layoffs were avoided.

Another high-performance or *high-involvement* organization is the Saturn Division, formed by General Motors in the 1980s (Appelbaum and Batt, 1994; Charles and Bennett, 1993). The United Auto Workers Union (UAW) advised on equipment and plant layout; teams of plant managers, workers, and UAW officials visited 60 benchmark companies around the world. The goal was to manufacture high-quality cars that could compete with the best in the moderate-price niche, and Saturn's vehicles succeeded on both counts. All production workers are trained in group problem solving, technical skills, and quality assurance methods.

Saturn is organized around self-managed teams that deal with workflow, quality, and personnel (teams devise their own absentee policies and hire workers). Throughout the plant, problem-solving groups of managers and workers specifically focus on improving production processes and quality. At the company level, Saturn management and the UAW jointly determine operational plans. Wages are received as an annual salary, set at 80 percent of the industry average. Another 20 percent is added if performance goals are met (including customer satisfaction), and up to 20 percent more for exceeding the goals. Job security is promised unless the market drastically erodes.

Not all high involvement companies are large. Johnsonville Sausage, for instance, organized its 600 production workers into self-directed teams. They deal with hiring, firing, quality control, problem solving on operations, identifying and resolving issues with suppliers, and reviewing customer complaints and modifying the product accordingly. Every worker is broadly trained and participates in instructing new hires. An evaluation system, also managed by a team, allocates the sizable profit-sharing bonuses (Stayer, 1990).

The author recently visited a five-employee firm that tests products for manufacturers. Each employee received training in technical skills and statistical process control, and at least once a week the group met for an hour to resolve any operational problems. Due to its excellent reputation for accurate testing, the business has prospered. Jobs are secure, and a profit-sharing plan is in place. That company, of course, provides a service. So does the Shenandoah Life Insurance Company, whose offices at several sites are nearly supervisor-free. Self-directed groups are responsible for the workflow and personnel matters, and extensive cross-training is tied to a pay-for-learning compensation plan (Appelbaum and Batt, 1994). Similarly effective change efforts can be found among department stores, hotels, and phone companies (Schlesinger and Heskitt, 1991; U.S. Congress, 1993). Along with manufacturers, therefore, service-industry organizations (both unionized and nonunion) may adopt practices that raise efficiency and have positive results for employees' jobs and incomes.

Dilemmas nevertheless have emerged in high-performance workplaces. Like most U.S. business organizations, which have primarily focused on cutting costs, companies that have embarked on transformation to high performance also have this concern. In these firms, restructuring and layoffs can occur together. The GTE Corporation (a regional phone company), for instance, introduced its long-range strategy of comprehensive cross-training, teamwork, and performance-based compensation and simultaneously announced the dismissal of thousands of employees (GTE Corporation, 1994). High-performance firms such as GTE, however, that seriously invest in training and reorganize work to gain efficiencies, then can stabilize or even increase employment in promising business units ("Why Downsizing," 1994). Still, if a prolonged downturn in the business occurs, it is unlikely to remain a safe haven for employees.

Obstacles

Though high-involvement companies are not a cure-all, their competitive strengths are far beyond the limits of the cost-cutting strategy.

Nevertheless the high-performance approach is often rejected because transformation is slow (five years is common), expensive (due to the cost of training, new equipment, and slowed output during the transition), and resisted by some employees (for fear of loss of current advantages). Moreover, the outcomes are fuzzy; efficiency, quality, and profitability elude precise forecasting. The low-wage path may thus seem more inviting than dealing with these obstacles. There are other hindrances, too. America's institutional context generally discourages investing in organizational transformation to high performance.

Major changes consume resources. Instead of producing consistently higher earnings or larger dividend payouts, time and money are expended on equipment, training, and so on. Investors may be displeased, a risk for firms. One solution, mentioned earlier, is business groups. Another is tax incentives that reward long-term stockholding. A remedy, in any event, is needed to gain investors' support for long-term competitive strategies.

In an economy with low union density, employers are attracted to the low-wage path. (The boomerang effect is that this also dampens workers' collective purchasing power and thereby economic activity.) With fewer unionized workplaces, there is little organized opposition to wage-trimming policies. When competing against lower-pay firms in the United States or elsewhere, employers are tempted to economize on wages.

Savings in employees' medical and retirement plans (neither of which is federally mandated) are also available. In 1980, over 70 percent of full-time workers in companies with 100-plus employees were covered by employer-paid health insurance; 10 years later it is around 30 percent, and less among smaller companies (Scofea, 1994). In these same years retirement programs also slipped. About 40 percent of the private-sector workforce is currently covered by a pension plan—mostly 401(k) plans funded partly or totally by employee contributions ("Harsh Medicine," 1994). The 401(k) system is a "defined contribution" program. Unlike the earlier "defined benefit" plans, which are legally binding on the employer and federally insured in the event of bankruptcy, in a defined contribution plan the retirement income is unpredictable. It depends on the success of the investments that the contributions have bought.

Job training—or more accurately, the lack of training—is also troublesome. While college graduates are readily available in a large variety of fields, skilled high school graduates are not. There is no American equivalent of Germany's apprenticeship system. Nearly 80 percent of young people in Germany who are not bound for college become apprentices in one of nearly 400 white- or blue-collar occupations. Combining on-the-job training with formal schooling equips trainees with both practical and theoretical understandings of a trade. During the three or four years of training, participants receive wages from their employers, and after a final examination they are qualified for journeyman's pay. The curriculum for each occupation is approved by national bodies of industry and commerce to which all firms must belong ("Germany," 1992–93). For school dropouts or failed apprentices, the Ministry of Labor offers remedial training courses to help them qualify for journeyman status.

Germany's apprenticeships are a national commitment. Most other industrialized nations, with the exception of the United States, also invest heavily in the skills of their young people who do not have college training (Thurow, 1992). As a result, many Americans drift from one low-wage job to another, without transportable training and often without the literacy or math skills to benefit from it. This competitive disadvantage raises training costs for would-be high-involvement companies. Improvement of education and vocational training has been taken on mostly at the state and local levels (Rzonca, Gustafson, and Boutelle, 1995). The national will and purse to do this have been absent.[10]

For a variety of reasons, then, employers may stay on the low-wage path rather than risking scarce resources to develop high-performance workplaces. Texeira and Mishel (1995, p. 194) sum up the stumbling blocks as "management myopia and fear of empowering workers; the lack of significant wage pressure; the ease of pursuing alternative low-wage options (producing offshore, depressing wages, benefits, and working conditions); and a variety of institutional barriers to change."

Global Reach

The Compaq Computer Company buys laptops and home PCs engineered and manufactured in Taiwan ("Where Compaq's Kingdom," 1995). The Johnson and Johnson Company has a pharmaceutical research and production joint venture in mainland China. The Ford Motor Company produces cars in Europe and Mexico and operates a credit subsidiary in Japan. U.S. West and its local partners are building a digital phone system in Russia and India and cable systems in Poland. Over 70 percent of the Gillette Company's sales revenues are from outside the United States, while American Telephone and Telegraph, in a network of affiliated firms, employs 50,000 persons in 90 countries (Annual reports for 1994, J&J, Ford, Gillette, AT&T; for 1992, U.S. West). In endless variety, American producers of goods and services are reaching out. At the same time, others are reaching in.

---

[10]A reasonable estimate is that half the young Americans from schools in the poorest neighborhoods are unemployable except in the lowest-paying jobs.

Mercedes, for instance, shed 20 percent of its workforce in Germany, organized team production, wrested pay concessions, and nonetheless will build a plant in the United States ("Germany Making Comeback," 1995).[11] The comparatively lower compensation of American workers is one lure to the many foreign companies that operate in this country.

But offshore units are not only a means to restrain costs. Most service firms, for example, must be present in a market if they want its customers. The ServiceMaster Company, with businesses in pest control and lawn, office, and home maintenance, must be on site in foreign markets. Even with manufactured products that can be exported, there are reasons for American firms to have facilities in external markets:

1. They provide a hedge against a downturn in the domestic economy. If U.S. sales are ailing, foreign markets may be robust.
2. Protectionist barriers are often lower for products made locally than for imports.
3. Currency swings can be countered. If the dollar should steeply rise (as Japan's yen has in the 1990s), America's exports would suffer. Buying materials and hiring labor in the local currency allows finished products to be sold in that currency and thus not priced out of the market.
4. Proximity to a market enhances understanding of the tastes and needs of local buyers.
5. A company and its products are more likely to be accepted if it uses local workers and suppliers.

Americans indeed have invested globally, as foreigners have invested in this country. However, by the end of the 1980s, the United States was a net debtor—more American assets were owned by foreigners than foreign assets were owned by Americans. In addition to operating businesses in the United States, thus sending profits overseas, foreigners hold roughly a trillion dollars of the federal debt. Add a persistent trade deficit, and the outflow of dollars is massive. The result is a falling dollar relative to other major currencies. A slumping dollar is wonderful for U.S. exports because they are cheaper in relation to others' products, and this boosts export-related jobs. A weak dollar might also provide an especially strong lever for prying open reluctant markets (Japan's, for example). But a sagging dollar is unfortunate for American investors because overseas assets became more expensive. Of course, the opposite

---

[11]The United Kingdom and Japan, followed by the Netherlands, have the largest direct investments in the United States. The total direct investment by all countries is nearly half a trillion dollars ("Vital Signs," 1994).

is also true. The United States attracted more direct foreign investment in the mid-1990s than any other country—foreign investors built plants here and bought American companies ("Suddenly, It's Time," 1995). A weakened dollar yields a mix of consequences. Some of these may be favorable, but they are eclipsed by the economic drag of the underlying causes.

Other industrialized countries have financial troubles, too. Most have budget deficits that are proportionately larger than the American one (though this country has accumulated a bigger federal debt). As a percent of gross domestic product in 1994, Germany's deficit of nearly 3 percent topped America's 2 percent, while deficits in France, Canada, Britain, and Italy ranged from three to five times the U.S. rate ("Deepest in the Hole," 1995). Sweden led the field with a deficit of 13 percent and a shrinking economy ("Swedish Economy," 1994). Slight net employment growth in EU countries, combined with large social expenditures, drove up the deficits, despite substantially higher taxes than in the United States ("Why the Cry," 1995). Predictions are that Japan also will borrow heavily.[12]

The Twenty-first Century

The U.S. Department of Labor forecasts no significant shifts of the workforce among occupations (Silvestri, 1993).[13] From now to 2005, expansion of professional and managerial occupations will be balanced by more service-worker and low-skill occupations. Also, no upgrading of educational requirements is expected—the pace of job growth among occupations that require college graduates will be about the same as for occupations that do not. Graduates, however, may enjoy increasingly larger payoffs. Some analysts expect a broader earnings gap between persons with college degrees and those without them, thus magnifying the current income disparities (American Society for Training, 1991).

Not everyone agrees with these predictions, however. The Hudson Institute's widely cited *Workforce 2000* (Johnston and Packer, 1987) offers this alternative view. In the years ahead, if stiffer competition is encouraged by removing existing trade barriers, expanding deregulation, and privatizing wherever possible, market forces will push firms to adopt the most efficient processes. In this more-demanding environment, skill requirements will move up, and output per worker will increase. Productivity gains will be reflected in rising wage levels. But critics distrust

---

[12]It may be necessary for Japan's Ministry of Finance to subsidize Japanese banks' failed real estate loans and to stimulate the Japanese economy if it remains sluggish.
[13]Periodically, the U.S. Labor Department issues pessimistic, optimistic, and midrange scenarios. The middle forecast is described here.

the assumptions that harsher competition lifts skill requirements and that the profits from improved productivity would be shared (DiTomaso and Friedman, 1995). So far, the evidence supports the skeptics.

On a larger scale of place and time, observers point to a gradually narrowing wage gap between the industrialized and developing countries. Average labor compensation costs in Taiwan, Singapore, and South Korea, for instance, have climbed to roughly 30 percent of the U.S. level and continue to rise. Now only a few products (airliners, for instance) cannot be designed and built in these developing nations and others. As Stewart (1994) notes,

> ...the new international division of labor is...associated with a new distribution of income. The division between rich and poor may no longer occur on country lines, but on class and skill lines. The poor of the world are to be found on the streets of London, Paris and New York, as well as Calcutta and Mexico City. (p. 29)

Scattered, too, are the prosperous executives and professionals who benefit from the global economy. They may have more in common with their international counterparts than with ordinary persons in their home countries.[14]

While developed and developing countries are slowly moving toward similar wages for similar skills, in some undeveloped countries living standards are drifting further down. Especially troubling are large areas of Africa—Somalia, Ethiopa, Zaire, Rwanda, and most of West Africa (Kaplan, 1994). African economies on average shrank 1 percent a year over the past decade: "In state after state, public institutions have collapsed, health care has diminished, infrastructure has fallen into disrepair and poverty has deepened" ("Zaire," 1994, p. A24). In the Cold War, both sides gave economic aid to African countries and backed friendly leaders; this interest and assistance have disappeared. The sources of decline range across tribal conflicts, crime, disease, overpopulation, and corrupt politicians. Turnarounds among Africa's weakened economies are not in sight. Nonetheless, forecasts about Africa have often been wrong.

The same caveat applies to the United States. It was widely thought that unemployment would soar when the men in uniform came home at the end of World War II. Instead, Americans broadly shared in three decades of rising prosperity. Perhaps the years ahead hold similar surprises.

---

[14]Robert Reich (1992, ch. 23) cautions that wealthy Americans are withdrawing from involvement in civic matters. With ample resources of their own, their lives are sheltered from reliance on public services or exposure to social problems.

References

Aaron, B. (1967). Regulation of internal union relations. In E. W. Bakke, C. Kerr, & C. W. Anrod (eds.), *Unions, Management, and the Public*, pp. 677–681. New York: Harcourt, Brace and World.

Adams, C., Bartley, P., Bourdillon, H., & Loxton, C. (1990). *From Workshop to Warfare: The Lives of Medieval Women*. New York: Cambridge University Press.

Adams, R. (1995). Industrial relations in Europe and North America. *European Journal of Industrial Relations, 1* (March): 47–62.

American Society for Training and Development (1991). *America and the New Economy*. Alexandria, VA.

Anderson, H. (1980). *Primer of Labor Relations*. Washington, DC: Bureau of National Affairs.

Antonio, R. J. (1979). Domination and production in bureaucracy. *American Sociological Review, 44*, 895–912.

Applebaum, E., & Batt, R. (1993). American models of high-performance work systems. *Workplace Topics, 3* (September): 67–99.

Applebaum, E., & Batt, R. (1994). *The New American Workplace*. Ithaca, NY: Cornell University, ILR Press.

Applebaum, H. (1992). *The Concept of Work: Ancient, Medieval, and Modern*. Albany: State University of New York Press.

Aronson, R. L. (1991). *Self-Employment*. Ithaca, NY: Cornell University, ILR Press.

Ashton, T. S. (1969). *The Industrial Revolution*. New York: Oxford University Press.

Barbash, J. (1980). Collective bargaining: Contemporary American experience. In G. G. Somers (ed.), *Collective Bargaining: Contemporary American Experience*, pp. 553–588. Madison: Industrial Relations Research Association, University of Wisconsin.

Barkin, S. (1991). Pure and simple unionism: An adequate base for union growth? In G. Strauss, D. G. Gallagher, & J. Fiorito (eds.), *The State of the Unions*, pp. 353–360. Madison: Industrial Relations Research Association, University of Wisconsin.

Baxter, J. (1994). Is husband's class enough? *American Sociological Review, 59*, 220–235.

Bell, D. (1975). *The Coming of Post-Industrial Society*. New York: Basic Books.

Berg, I. (1979). *Industrial Sociology*. Englewood Cliffs, NJ: Prentice-Hall.

Best, G. (1972). *Mid-Victorian Britain, 1851–1875*. New York: Schocken Books.

Bose, C. E., & Rossi, P. H. (1983). Gender and jobs: Prestige standings of occupations as affected by gender. *American Sociological Review, 4*, 316–330.

Bower, B. (1992a). Erectus unhinged. *Science News, 141*, 408–409, 411.

Bower, B. (1992b). Hammer time in the Stone Age. *Science News, 142*, 428.

Boyett, J. H., & Conn, H. (1992). *Workplace 2000*. New York: Plume.

Braidwood, R. J., & Dyson, R. H. (1968). Domestication. In *International Encyclopedia of the Social Sciences* (Vol. 4, pp. 245–254). New York: Macmillan and Free Press.

Braudel, F. (1973). *Capitalism and Material Life, 1400–1800*, trans. M. Kochan. New York: Harper & Row.

Braverman, H. (1974). *Labor and Monopoly Capital*. New York: Monthly Review Press.

Brayfield, A. H., & Crockett, J. H. (1995). Employee attitudes and employee performance. *Psychological Bulletin, 52*, 284–290.

Bronfenbrenner, M., Sichel, W., & Gardner, W. (1987). *Macroeconomics*, 2nd ed. Boston: Houghton Mifflin.

Butler, R., & Heckman, J. J. (1977). The government's impact on the labor market status of black Americans. In L. J. Hausman, O. Ashenfelter, B. Rustin, R. F. Schubert, & D. Slaiman (eds.), *Equal Rights and Industrial Relations*, pp. 235–281. Madison: Industrial Relations Research Association, University of Wisconsin.

Cameron, K. S., Freeman, S. J., & Mishra, A. K. (1993). Downsizing and redesigning organizations. In G. Huber and W. H. Glick (eds.), *Organizational Change and Redesign*, pp. 19–65. New York: Oxford University Press.

Carey, A. (1967). The Hawthorne studies: A radical criticism. *American Sociological Review, 32*, 403–416.

Carneiro, R. L. (1970). A theory of the origin of the state. *Science, 169*, 733–738.

Carre, F. J. (1992). Temporary employment in the eighties. In V. L. duRivage (ed.), *New Policies for the Part-Time and Contingent Workforce*, pp. 45–87. Armonk, NY: Sharp.

Cattan, B. (1993). The diversity of Hispanics in the U.S. work force. *Monthly Labor Review, 116* (8): 3–15.

Chaison, G. N., & Dhavale, D. G. (1990). A note on the severity of the decline in union organizing activity. *Industrial and Labor Relations Review, 43*, 366–373.

Chaison, G. N., & Rose, J. B. (1991). The macrodeterminants of union growth and decline. In G. Strauss, D. G. Gallagher, & J. Fiorito (eds.), *The State of the Unions*, pp. 3–46. Madison: Industrial Relations Research Association, University of Wisconsin.

Chandler, A. D., Jr. (1977). The structure of American industry in the twentieth century: a historical overview. In E. J. Perkins (ed.), *Men and Organizations*, pp. 26–37. New York: G. Putnam's Sons.

Charles, H., & Bennett, M. E. (1993). Union-management partnership in the application of technology: Saturn Corporation-UAW Local 1853. *Workplace Topics, 3* (September): 113–122.

Childe, G. V. (1964). *What Happened in History*. Baltimore: Penguin Books.

Clawson, D. (1980). *Bureaucracy and the Labor Process*. New York: Monthly Review Press.

Colclough, G., & Tolbert, C. M. (1992). *Work in the Fast Lane*. Albany: State University of New York Press.

Coleman, J. S. (1974). *Power and the Structure of Society*. New York: Norton.

Coleman, J. S., Campbell, E. Q., Hobson, C. J., McPartland, J., Mood, A. M., Weinfeld, F. D., & York, R. L. (1966). *Equality of Educational Opportunity*. Washington, DC.

Collins, R. (1975). *Conflict Sociology*. New York: Academic Press.

Connor, J. E. (ed.) (1968). *Lenin on Politics and Revolution, Selected Writings*. New York: Pegasus Books.

Damus, J. (1968). *The Middle Ages*. Garden City, NY: Image Books.

Dating an ancient Russian revolution (1993). *Science News, 144* (October 2): 217.

Davis, J. A., & Smith, T. (1994). *General Social Surveys, 1972–1994: Cumulative Codebook*. Chicago: National Opinion Research Center.

Davis, J. P. (1961). *Corporations*. New York: Capricorn Books.

Davis, K., & Moore, W. (1945). Some principles of stratification. *American Sociological Review, 10*, 242–249.

Deepest in the hole (1995). *Business Week*, January 23, p. 8.

Deliver—or else (1995). *Business Week*, March 27, pp. 36–38.

Derber, C., Schwartz, W. A., & Magrass, Y. (1990). *Power in the Highest Degree: Professionals and the Rise of a New Mandarin Order*. New York: Oxford University Press.

Didrichsen, J. (1977). The development of diversified and conglomerate firms in the United States, 1920–1970. In E. J. Perkins (ed.), *Men and Organizations*, pp. 38–50. New York: G. Putnam's Sons.

DiTomaso, N. D., & Friedman, J. J. (1995). A sociological commentary on workforce 2000. In D. B. Bills (ed.), *The New Modern Times*, pp. 207–233. Albany: State University of New York Press.

Doeringer, P. B., & Piore, M. J. (1971). *Internal Labor Markets and Manpower Analysis*. Lexington, MA: D. C. Heath.

Douglas, J. M. (1994). The legality of faculty-shared governance in light of Electromation, DuPont, and a revisited Yeshiva. *Workplace Topics, 4* (June): 45–60.

Employee tenure and occupational mobility in the early 1990s (1992). U.S. Department of Labor, Bureau of Labor Statistics, *News*, June 26.

Employment and earnings characteristics of families: Fourth Quarter, 1993 (1994). U.S. Department of Labor, Bureau of Labor Statistics, *News*, February 1.

Employment situation, The: February 1994 (1994). U.S. Department of Labor, Bureau of Labor Statistics, *News*, March 4.

Employment situation, The: November 1993 (1993). U.S. Department of Labor, Bureau of Labor Statistics, *News*, December 3.

Employment situation, The: May 1994 (1994). U.S. Department of Labor, Bureau of Labor Statistics, *News*, June 3.

England, P. (1992) *Comparable Worth: Theories and Evidence*. New York: Aldine DeGruyter.

Erikson, R., & Goldthorpe, J. H. (1993). *The Constant Flux: A Study of Class Mobility in Industrial Societies*. New York: Oxford University Press.

Europe's high taxes climb (1995). *Business Week*, March 13, p. 26.

Experimenting with test tube temps. *U.S. News and World Report*, October 11, 1993, p. 70.

Eyeball to eyeball with China (1995). *Business Week*, February, 20, pp. 32–33.

Fakhry, A. (1961). *The Pyramids*. Chicago. University of Chicago Press.

Featherman, D. L., & Hauser, R. M. (1978). *Opportunity and Change*. New York: Academic Press.

Finucane, R. S. (1983). *Soldiers of the Faith: Crusaders and Moslems at War*. New York: St. Martin's Press.

Freeman, R. B. (1994). How labor fares in advanced economies. In R. B. Freeman (ed.), *Working under Different Rules* (pp. 1–28). New York: Russell Sage Foundation.

Furnham, A. (1990). *The Protestant Work Ethic*. New York: Routledge.

Gap in wealth in U.S. called widest in West (1995). *New York Times*, April 17, pp. A1, D4.

Germany (1992–93). In U.S. Department of Labor, *Foreign Labor Trends*, FLT 94–17. Washington, DC.

Germany making comeback, with Daimler in the lead (1995). *The Wall Street Journal*, April 7, p. A10.

Gillespie, R. (1991). *Manufacturing Knowledge*. New York: Cambridge University Press.

Ginzberg, E., & Berman, H. (1964). *The American Worker in the Twentieth Century*. New York: Free Press.

Gold, M. E. (1989). *An Introduction to Labor Law*. Ithaca, NY: Cornell University, ILR Press.

Gold, M. E. (1993). *An Introduction to the Law of Employment Discrimination*. Ithaca, NY: Cornell University, ILR Press.

Gompers, S. (1919). *Labor and the Common Welfare*. New York: Dutton.

Gould, W. B. (1993). *A Primer on American Labor Law*, 3rd ed. Cambridge, MA: MIT Press.

GTE Corporation (1994). *Annual Report*. Stamford, CT.

Gutman, H. (1977). *Work, Culture and Society in Industrializing America*. New York: Vintage Books.

Hall, R. (1994). *Sociology of Work*. Thousand Oaks, CA: Pine Forge Press.

Hall, W. P., & Albion, R. G. (1953). *A History of England and the British Empire*. New York: Ginn.

Haller, M., Konig, W., Krause, P., & Kurz, K. (1985). Patterns of career mobility and structural positions in advanced capitalist societies: A comparison of men in Austria, France, and the United States. *American Sociological Review, 50*, 579–603.

Hammer, M., & Champy, J. (1993). *Reengineering the Corporation*. New York: HarperCollins.

Harrison, B. (1994). *Lean and Mean: The Changing Landscape of Corporate Power*. New York: Basic Books.

Harsh medicine for ailing pension plans (1994). *Business Week*, September 19, pp. 91–94.

Hauser, R. M., & Featherman, D. L. (1977). *The Process of Stratification*. New York: Academic Press.

Heckscher, C., & Donnellon, A. (eds.) (1994). *The Post-Bureaucratic Organization*. Thousand Oaks, CA: Sage.

Help wanted for less pay (1995). *Business Week*, May 8, p. 28.

Herzberg, F. (1968). One more time: How do you motivate employees? *Harvard Business Review, 46* (January-February): 53–62.

Hodson, R., & Kaufman, R. L. (1982). Economic dualism: A critical review. *American Sociological Review, 47*, 727–739.

Hodson, R., & Sullivan, T. A. (1995). *The Social Organization of Work*, 2nd ed. Belmont, CA: Wadsworth.

Hogler, R., & Grenier, G. J. (1992). *Employee Participation and Labor Law in the American Workplace*. New York: Quorum Books.

Holstein, W. J. (1994). In Japan. *Business Week*, August 8, pp. 38–39.

Homans, G. (1961). *Social Behavior: Its Elementary Forms.* New York: Harcourt, Brace & World.

Hout, M. (1988). More universalism, less structural mobility: The American occupational structure in the 1980s. *American Journal of Sociology, 93,* 1358–1400.

It's a small (business) world (1995). *Business Week,* April 17, pp. 96–101.

Jackall, R. (1988). *Moral Mazes: The World of Corporate Managers.* New York: Oxford University Press.

Jacoby, H. (1973). *The Bureaucratization of the World,* trans. E. Kanes, Berkeley: University of California Press.

Job drought, The (1992). *Fortune,* August 24, pp. 62–74.

Job woes in the Group of Seven (1994). *New York Times,* March 14, p. D6.

Johnston, W. B., & Packer, A. H. (1987). *Workforce 2000: Work and Workers for the 21st Century.* Indianapolis: Hudson Institute.

Kahn, R. L. (1974). The work module. In J. O'Toole (ed.), *Work and the Quality of Life,* pp. 199–226. Cambridge, MA: MIT Press.

Kamata, S. (1982). *Japan in the Passing Lane,* trans. T. Akimoto. New York: Pantheon.

Kanter, R. M. (1993). *Men and Women of the Corporation,* rev. ed. New York: Basic Books.

Kaplan, R. D. (1994). The coming anarchy. *The Atlantic Monthly,* February, pp. 44–76.

Katzenstein, G. (1989). *Funny Business: An Outsider's Year in Japan.* Englewood Cliffs, NJ: Prentice-Hall.

Kochan, T. A., & Osterman, P. (1991). *The Mutual Gains Enterprise.* Boston, MA: Harvard Business School.

Kochan, T. A., & Wever, K. R. (1994). American unions and the future of worker representation. In G. Strauss, D. G. Gallagher, & J. Fiorito (eds.), *The State of the Unions,* pp. 363–386. Madison: Industrial Relations Research Association, University of Wisconsin.

Kirsch, D. (1978). *Financial and Economic Journalism.* New York: New York University Press.

Kranzberg, M., & Gies, J. (1975). *By the Sweat of Thy Brow.* New York: G. Putnam's Sons.

Krecker, M. L. (1994). Work careers and organizational careers. *Work and Occupations, 21* (August): 251–283.

LaFay, H. (1978). Ebla. *National Geographic, 154,* 730–759.

Lawler, E. E. (1990) *Strategic pay.* San Francisco: Jossey-Bass.

Lawler, E. E., Mohrman, S. A., & Ledford, G. E. (1992). *Employee Involvement and Total Quality Management.* San Francisco: Jossey-Bass.

Lehmann, S. G. (1995). Costs and opportunities of marketization: An analysis of Russian employment and unemployment. In R. L. Simpson & I. H. Simpson (eds.), *Research in the Sociology of Work,* Vol. 5, *The meanings of work,* pp. 205–233. Greenwich, CT: Jai Press.

Leidner, R. (1993). *Fast Food, Fast Talk: Service Work and the Routinization of Everyday Life.* Berkeley: University of California Press.

Lenski, G. E. (1966). *Power and Privilege.* New York: McGraw-Hill.

Lenski, G. E., & Lenski, J. (1982). *Human Societies.* New York: McGraw-Hill.

Levitan, S. (1961). An appraisal of the anti-trust approach. *The Annals, 33,* 108–118.

Lewis, M. (1993), *The Culture of Inequality,* 2nd ed. Amherst: University of Massachusetts Press.

Lewis, W. H. (1957). *The Splendid Century: Life in the France of Louis XIV.* Garden City, NY: Anchor Books.

Lincoln, J. R., & Kalleberg, A. L. (1990). *Culture, Control, and Commitment: A Study of Work Organization and Work Attitudes in the United States and Japan.* New York: Cambridge University Press.

Lincoln, J. R., & McBride, K. (1987). Japanese industrial organization in comparative perspective. In W. R. Scott & J. F. Short (eds.), *Annual Review of Sociology,* pp. 289–312. Palo Alto, CA: Annual Reviews.

Linton, R. (1955). *The Tree of Culture.* New York: Alfred A. Knopf.

Lipset, S. M., & Bendix, R. (1959). *Social Mobility in Industrial Society.* Berkeley: University of California Press.

Maine, H. S. (1906). *Ancient Law.* New York: Henry Holt.

Manchester, W. (1993). *A World Lit Only by Fire: The Medieval Mind and the Renaissance.* New York: Little, Brown.

Mantoux, P. (1961). *The Industrial Revolution in the Eighteenth Century.* New York: Harper & Row.

Markoff, J. (1995). Where the chips may fall. *The New York Times,* April 17, pp. D1, D7.

Martin, J. K., & Miller, G. A. (1986). Job satisfaction and absenteeism: Organizational, individual, and job-related correlates. *Work and Occupations, 13* (February): 33–46.

Marx, Karl (1906). *Capital,* Vol. 1, trans. S. Moore and E. Aveling. London: Charles Kerr. (Originally published 1867)

Maslow, A. H. (1965). *Eupsychian Management.* Homewood, IL: Richard D. Irwin.

McGregor, D. (1957). The human side of enterprise. *Management Review, 46,* 22–28, 88–92.

Mesopotamia (1981). In J. A. Garrity and P. Gay (eds.), *The Columbia History of the World,* pp. 49–67. New York: Dorset Press.

Mishel, L., & Bernstein, J. (1993). *The State of Working America, 1992–93.* Armonk, NY: Sharpe.

Montgomery, D. (1976). American labor, 1865–1902. *Monthly Labor Review, 99,* 10–17.

Mowday, R. T., Porter, L. W., & Steers, R. (1982). *Employee-Organization Linkages: The Psychology of Commitment, Absenteeism, and Turnover.* New York: Academic Press.

Neff, R. (1995). Commentary: Why Japanese deregulation won't much help America. *Business Week,* April 3, p. 72.

New export champs, The (1986). *The New York Times,* December 7, p. D1.

New Levant, The (1981). In J. A. Garrity and P. Gay (eds.), *The Columbia History of the World,* pp. 82–90. New York: Dorset Press.

O.K., back to work (1993). *Business Week,* December 20, pp. 34–35.

Okita, S. (1985). Economic planning in Japan. In L. Thurow (ed.), *The Management Challenge,* pp. 191–217. Cambridge, MA: MIT Press.

Parsons, H. W. (1974). What really happened at Hawthorne? *Science, 183,* 922–932.

Peterson, W. H. (1986). Why not save the 31,000 top farmers? *The Wall Street Journal,* October 8, p. 34.

Pfeiffer, J. E. (1977). *The Emergence of Society.* New York: McGraw-Hill.

Pinchot, G., & Pinchot, E. (1993). *The End of Bureaucracy and the Rise of the Intelligent Organization.* San Francisco: Berrett-Koehler.

Pinder, C. C. (1984). *Work Motivation.* Glenview, IL: Scott, Foresman.

Pirenne, H. (1955). *A History of Europe*, trans. B. Miall. New York: University Books.

Polanyi, K. (1957). *The Great Transformation*. Boston: Beacon Press.

Presser, H. B. (1994). Employment schedules among dual-earner spouses and the division of household labor by gender. *American Sociological Review, 59* (June): 348–364.

Real Earnings in August 1994. Department of Labor, Bureau of Labor Statistics, *News* July 13, 1994.

Reich, R. B. (1992). *The Work of Nations*. New York: Vintage Books.

Reskin, B., & Padavic, I. (1994). *Women and Men at Work*. Thousand Oaks, CA: Pine Forge Press.

Ricardo, David (1821). *On the Principles of Political Economy and Taxation*. Cambridge, England: Straffe.

Robbins, M. (1965). *The Railway Age in Britain*. Baltimore, MD: Penguin Books.

Robbins, S. (1994). *Essentials of Organization Behavior*, 4th ed. Englewood Cliffs, NJ: Prentice-Hall.

Roberts, D. (1994). Egypt's old kingdom. *National Geographic, 187* (January): 2–45.

Robinson, J. G., & McIlwee, J. S. (1989). Obstacles to unionization in high-tech industries. *Work and Occupations, 16*, 115–136.

Roethlisberger, F. J. (1941). *Management and Morale*. Cambridge, MA: Harvard University Press.

Roethlisberger, F. J., & Dickson, W. J. (1939). *Management and the Worker*. Cambridge, MA: Harvard University Press.

Rogers, J., & Streeck, W. (1994). Workplace representation overseas: The works council story. In R. B. Freeman (ed.), *Working under Different Rules*, pp. 97–156. New York: Russell Sage Foundation.

Ronan, W. W. (1970). Individual and situational variables relating to job satisfaction. *Journal of Applied Psychology Monograph*, Vol. 54, Part 2, pp. 1–31.

Roos, P. A. (1985). *Gender and Work: A Comparative Analysis of Industrial Societies*. Albany: State University of New York Press.

Ryscavage, P. (1979). More wives in the labor force have husbands with above-average incomes. *Monthly Labor Review, 102*, 25–30.

Rzonca, C., Gustafson, D., & Boutelle, S. (1995). Vocational education. In D. B. Bills (ed.), *The New Modern Times*, pp. 139–162. Albany: State University of New York Press.

Saint-Simon, Duc de, L. (1964). *The Age of Magnificence: Memoirs of the Court of Louis XIV*, ed. and trans. Sanche de Gramont. New York: Capricorn Books.

Saltzman, G. M. (1994). Job applicant screening by a Japanese transplant: A union-avoidance tactic. *Workplace Topics, 4* (June): 61–82.

Schlesinger, L. A., & Heskett, J. L. (1991). Enfranchisement of service workers. *California Management Review, 33* (Summer): 83–100.

Scofea, L. A. (1994). The development and growth of employer-provided health insurance. *Monthly Labor Review*, March, pp. 3–10.

Secret weapon that won't start a trade war, The (1994). *Business Week*, March 7, p. 45.

Seeds of warfare precede agriculture (1995). *Science News, 147* (January 7): 4.

Seligman, B. (1971). *The Potentates*. New York: Dial Press.

Sennett, R., & Cobb, R. (1973). *The Hidden Injuries of Class*. New York: Vintage Books.

Silvestri, G. T. (1993). Occupational employment. *Montly Labor Review* (November): 58–86.

Smelser, N. J. (1959). *Social Change in the Industrial Revolution*. Chicago: University of Chicago Press.

Smith, A. (1937). *The Wealth of Nations*. New York: Random House, Modern Library Edition. (Originally published 1776)

South, J. S., & Spitze, G. (1994). Housework in marital and nonmarital households. *American Sociological Review, 59* (June): 327–347.

Spitze, G. (1988). The data on women's labor force participation. In A. H. Stromberg & S. Harkess (eds.), *Women Working*, 2nd ed., pp. 42–60. Mountain View, CA: Mayfield.

Stark, D., & Nee, V. (1989). Toward an institutional analysis of state socialism. In V. Nee & D. Stark (eds.), *Remaking the Economic Institutions of Socialism: China and Eastern Europe*, pp. 1–31. Stanford, CA: Stanford University Press.

Stayer, R. (1990). How I learned to let my workers lead. *Harvard Business Review*, November-December, pp. 71–81.

Steers, R. M., & Porter, L. W. (eds.) (1987). *Motivation and Work Behavior*. New York: McGraw-Hill.

Steinberg, R. J. (1992). Gendered instructions. *Work and Occupations, 19*, 387–423.

Steinberg, R. J., & Cook, A. (1988). Policies affecting women's employment in industrial countries. In A. H. Stromberg & S. Harkess (eds.), *Women Working*, 2nd ed., pp. 307–328. Mountain View, CA: Mayfield.

Stern, J. L., & Johnson, D. B. (1968). *Blue- to White-Collar Mobility*. Madison: Industrial Relations Research Association, University of Wisconsin.

Sterngold, J. (1995). Do transit rail cars need U.S. label? *The New York Times*, April 4, p. D2.

Stewart, F. (1994). The new international division of labor. *World of Work, 8* (June 8): 28–29.

Suddenly it's time to buy American (1995). *Business Week*, March 27, p. 58.

Swedish economy, The (1994). *Facts Sheets on Sweden*. Stockholm: The Swedish Institute.

Symposium—The American occupational structure: Reflections after twenty-five years (1992). *Contemporary Sociology, 21* (September): 596–668.

Tausky, C. (1984). *Work and Society: An Introduction to Industrial Sociology*. Itasca, IL: F. E. Peacock.

Tausky, C. (1991). *Perestroika* in the USSR and China. *Work and Occupations, 18*, 94–108.

Tausky, C., & Parke, E. L. (1976). Job enrichment, need theory and reinforcement theory. In R. Dubin (ed.), *Handbook of Work, Organization, and Society*, pp. 531–565. Chicago: Rand McNally.

Taylor, F. W. (1947). *Scientific Management*. New York: Harper & Row. (Originally published 1911)

Teixeira, R. A., & Mishel, L. (1995). Skills shortage or management shortage? In D. B. Bills (ed.), *The New Modern Times*, pp. 193–205. Albany: State University of New York Press.

That eye-popping executive pay (1994). *Business Week*, April 25, pp. 52–98.

Thompson, E. P. (1964). *The Making of the British Working Class*. New York: Pantheon Books.

Thurow, L. C. (1980). *The Zero-Sum Society*. New York: Penguin Books.

Thurow, L. C. (1992). Head to Head: The Coming Economic Battle Between Japan, Europe, and America. New York: Morrow.

Tomaskovic-Devey, D. (1993). *Gender and Racial Inequality at Work*. Ithaca, NY: School of Industrial and Labor Relations, Cornell University.

Treiman, Donald J. (1977). *Occupational Prestige in Comparative Perspective*. New York: Academic Press.

Triple Revolution, The (1994). *Business Week*, special issue, November 18, pp. 16–25.

Tuchman, B. W. (1978). *A Distant Mirror*. New York: Alfred A. Knopf.

Tumin, M. (1953). Some principles of stratification: A critical analysis. *American Sociological Review, 18*, 387–394.

Turner, L. (1994). Social partnership: An organizing concept for industrial relations reform. *Workplace Topics, 4* (June): 83–97.

United Nations (1973). *The Determinants and Consequences of Population Trends*, Vol. 1. New York.

U.S. Bureau of the Census (1975). *Historical Statistics of the United States, Colonial Times to 1970*, Bicentennial Edition, Part 2. Washington, DC.

U.S. Bureau of the Census, *Statistical Abstract of the United States* (1995). Washington, DC.

U.S. Congress, Office of Technology Assessment (1991). *Competing Economies*, OTA–ITE–498. Washington, DC.

U.S. Congress, Office of Technology Assessment (1993). *Pulling Together for Productivity: A Union-Management Experiment at U.S. West*. Washington, DC.

U.S. Department of Labor (1975a). *Handbook of Labor Statistics, 1975*, Reference Edition. Bureau of Labor Statistics, Bulletin 1865. Washington, DC.

U.S. Department of Labor (1975b). *Manpower Report of the President*. Washington, DC.

U.S. Department of Labor (1979). *A Century of Change in Boston Family Consumption Patterns*. Bureau of Labor Statistics, Regional Report No. 79–5. Washington, DC.

U.S. Department of Labor (1980). *Occupational Mobility during 1977*. Bureau of Labor Statistics, Special Labor Force Report No. 231. Washington, DC.

U.S. Department of Labor (1991). *A Report on the Glass Ceiling Initiative*. Bureau of Labor Statistics. Washington, DC.

U.S. Department of Labor (1994). Bureau of Labor Statistics, *Employment and Earnings, 41* (January).

Usual weekly earnings of wage and salary workers: Third quarter 1994 (1994). U.S. Department of Labor, Bureau of Labor Statistics, *News*, October 26.

van den Berghe, P. L. (1991). Sociology. In M. Maxwell (ed.), *The Sociological Imagination*, pp. 269–282. Albany: State University of New York Press.

Vital signs (1994). *Investor's Business Daily*, April 18, p. B1.

Vroom, Victor H. (1964). *Work and Motivation*. New York: John Wiley.

Walder, A. (1986). *Communist Neo-Traditionalism*. Berkeley: University of California Press.

Ware, N. (1964). *The Industrial Worker, 1840–1860*. Chicago: Quadrangle Books.

Weber, M. (1958). *The Protestant Ethic and the Spirit of Capitalism*, trans. T. Parsons. New York: Charles Scribner's Sons. (Originally published 1905)

Wellins, R. S., Byham, W. C., & Wilson, J. M. (1991). *Empowered Teams*. San Francisco: Jossey-Bass.

Western, M., & Wright, E. O. (1994). Class boundaries and intergenerational mobility among men. *American Sociological Review, 59* (August): 606–629.

Where Compaq's kingdom is weak (1995). *Business Week*, May 8, pp. 98–102.

White, L. (1962). *Medieval Technology and Social Change*. London: Oxford University Press.

White, male, and worried (1994). *Business Week*, January 31, pp. 50–55.

Whitehead, T. N. (1939). *The Industrial Worker*. Cambridge, MA: Harvard University Press.

Who we were: The origins of modern humans (1991). *U.S. News and World Report*, September, pp. 53–59.

Who'll get the lion's share of wealth in the '90s? The lions (1992). *Business Week*, June 8, pp. 86–88.

Why America needs unions (1994). *Business Week*, May 23, pp. 70–74, 78, 82.

Why downsizing looks different these days (1994). *Business Week*, October 10, p. 43.

Why the cry for tax relief? (1995). *Business Week*, January 23, p. 30.

Wittfogel, K. (1957). *Oriental Despotism*. New Haven, CT: Yale University Press.

Wolf, E. R. (1966). *Peasants*. Englewood Cliffs, NJ: Prentice-Hall.

Wolfbein, S. (1971). *Work in American Society*. Glenview, IL: Scott, Foresman.

Womack, J. P., Jones, D. T., & Roos, D. (1991). *The Machine That Changed the World: The Story of Lean Production*. New York: HarperCollins.

Worker displacement during the early 1990s (1994). *News*, September 14.

World Almanac and Book of Facts, The (1994, 1995). Mahwah, NJ: Funk & Wagnalls.

World Development Report, 1993 (1994). International Bank for Reconstruction and Development/World Bank. New York: Oxford University Press.

Yellowitz, I. (1969). *The Position of the Worker in American Society: 1865–1896*. Englewood Cliffs, NJ: Prentice-Hall.

Zaire (1994). *The Washington Post*, July 10, pp. A1, A24.

Index

Absenteeism, 78
Adams, Carol, 16
Adams, Roy G., 98
Adversarial relationships
  in income theory, 63–64
  in work outcomes, 84
Affirmative action, 51
Agricultural revolution, 4–5
Agriculture, 9–10, 13–14, 16, 36–37
Alexander the Great, 8, 12
American system of
      interchangeable parts, 35
Antonio, Robert J., 12
Appelbaum, Eileen, 115, 116
Applebaum, Herbert, 13, 14
Apprenticeship
  in Germany, 119–120
  in Middle Ages, 18–19
  in United States, 119
Arkwright's frame, 25, 35
Ashton, T.S., 1, 24, 27
AT&T Company, 120

Barbash, Jack, 97
Barkin, Solomon, 98
Batt, Rosemary, 115, 116
Bell, Daniel, 106
Bendix, Reinhard, 86
Benefits (see Medical insurance
      plans; Retirement plans)
Berg, Ivar, 24
Best, Geoffrey, 31, 33

Bose, Christine, 74
Boyett, Joseph H., 116, 117
Braudel, Fernand, 15
Braverman, Harry, 20
Brayfield, Arthur H., 77
Business groups (see also Keiretsu),
      111–112

Canals, in industrialization, 27, 36
Child labor
  in Industrial Revolution, 30–31
  in putting-out system, 21
Childe, V. Gordon, 7, 8
China, 24, 110–111
Clawson, Dan, 40
Colclough, Glenna, 115
Coleman, James S., 38, 75
Collective bargaining (see also Labor
      unions)
  in England, 33
  in United States, 41, 84, 98–102
College graduates
  by race and gender (table), 52
Collins, Randall, 64
Command economies, 110–111
Concentration of production, 36–37,
      37–39, 64–65
Conflict theory, 64
Contingent workers, 58–59
Cook, Alice, 46
Crockett, James, H., 77
Crusades, 16

Damus, Joseph, 15
Davis, John, 18, 19
Davis, Kingsley, 63
Didrichsen, Jon, 39
Domestic servants
    in England, 33
    in United States, 34, (tables) 48,
        50, 58
Domestic system (*see* Putting-out
        system)

Education (*see also* College graduates)
    and income, 49
    and occupational mobility, 87, 89, 122
Egypt
    organization of, 9, 10, 12
    pyramid construction in, 10, 11
Employee associations (*see* Labor
        unions)
Erikson, Robert, 86, 88, 89

Factory system (*see also* Industrial
        Revolution)
    origins in England, 22, 24–27
    in United States, 34–46
Featherman, David, 87, 88
Federal Reserve Board, 108, 114
Feudal system, 15
Ford, Henry (*see* Ford Motor
        Company)
Ford Motor Company, 40–41, 120

General Agreement on Tariffs and
        Trade (GATT), 108
Gies, Joseph, 3, 11
Gillespie, Richard, 77
Gillette Company, 120
Ginzberg, Eli, 41
Gold, Michael E., 93, 99
Goldthorpe, John H., 86, 88, 89
Gompers, Samuel, 98
Gould, William B., 101
Gross National Product, 24
GTE Corporation, 118
Guild system
    in Middle Ages, 17–20
    in Rome, 12–13
Gutman, Herbert, 2

Hall, Richard H., 63, 64, 80
Harrison, Bennett, 111

Hauser, Robert, 87, 88
Hawthorne experiments, 76
Heckscher, Charles, 116
Herzberg, Frederick, 76
High-performance firms
    characteristics of, 116
    examples of, 117–118
    obstacles to, 118–120
Hodson, Randy, 64, 79
Hominids, 2–3
Homo sapiens, 3
Human relations theory, 76–77
Hunting-gathering, 2–4

Immigration to America, 34
Incentives (*see also* Productivity), 77,
        81–82
Income
    distributions (tables), 66–74
    theories of, 61–66
Incorporation (*see* Limited liability)
Industrial Revolution
    advantages of, 23–24
    in England, 24–34
    in United States, 34–43
Industrial sociology, defined, 2
Industrialization (*see* Factory system;
        Industrial Revolution)
Industries (table), 57
Iron, 8, 9, 26
"Iron law of wages" (*see* Ricardo,
        David)

Jackall, Robert, 79
Japan, 77, 111, 113
Job satisfaction (*see* Work
        satisfaction)
Johnson & Johnson Company, 120
Johnsonville Sausage Company, 118

Kahn, Robert L., 79
Kalleberg, Arne L., 77, 80
Kanter, Rosabeth M., 39, 79
Keiretsu, 111–112
Kochan, Thomas, 103, 115
Kranzberg, Melvin, 3, 11

Labor force (*see also* Contingent
        workers)
    defined, 44
    participation rates (tables), 45, 47

Labor law, 90–95
Labor turnover, 84–85
Labor unions, 95–104
Lawler, Edward E., 78, 82
Leidner, Robin, 79
Lenin, praising scientific
     management, 40
Lenski, Gerhard, 5, 9
Lewis, Michael, 75
Limited liability, 37
Lincoln, James R., 80
Linton, Ralph, 11
Lipset, Seymour M., 86
Low-wage path, 115
Luther, Martin, 29

Management by objectives, 78
Manchester, William, 16
Manorial system, 14–17
Marx, Karl
     on revolution, 32
     on wages, 62
Maslow, Abraham, 76
McGregor, Douglas, 76
Medical insurance plans, 119
Mercantilism, 61, 111
Middle Ages, 14–22
Mishel, Lawrence, 120
Motorola Corporation, 117
Mowday, Richard T., 78

National Labor Relations Board (*see
     also* Labor law), 93–95,
     101–104

Occupational mobility
     in 19th century England, 33
     in United States, 84–89
Occupations
     labor force distributions (tables),
          48, 50
     in year 2000, 122–123
Organizations
     concentration of production,
          38–39
     by employee size class (table),
          59–60
Osterman, Paul, 115

Physiocrats (*see also* Income,
     theories of), 61

Pinchot, Elizabeth, 115
Pinchot, Gifford, 115
Pinder, Craig G., 78
Polanyi, Karl, 2
Porter, Lyman W., 75
Prestige
     consequences of, 74–75
     defined, 74
     explanations of, 74
Productivity
     and incentives, 78, 116
     and work satisfaction, 76–79
Proprietary theory of the state, 9
Protestant ethic, 29
Putting-out system, 20–23

Railroads
     in British industrialization, 27–28
     in American industrialization, 36
Retirement plans (defined
          benefits/contributions), 119
Ricardo, David, 62
Robbins, Stephen P., 78
Roethlisberger, Fritz J., 76
Roman Empire, 12–15
Ronan, W.W., 77
Roos, Patricia A., 89
Rossi, Peter H., 74

Saturn Division of General Motors,
     103, 117
Scientific management, 40, 77, 115
Self-employment, 59
Seligman, Ben B., 35, 36
Serfs, 9, 18, 74
Service industries, 51–54
ServiceMaster Company, 121
Shenandoah Life Insurance
     Company, 118
Slavery, 5, 8, 13, 34, 74
Smelser, Neal J., 31
Smith, Adam
     on pin making, 31–32
     on wages, 61
Sociobiology (*see also* Conflict
     theory), 64
Spitze, Glenna, 46
Steam engine, 26, 35
Steers, Richard M., 78
Steinberg, Ronnie J., 46
Stewart, Frances, 123

Sullivan, Teresa, 64, 79
Sumeria, 6–8

Taylor, Frederick, 40, 77, 115
Texeira, Ruy A., 120
Thurow, Lester, 106, 108, 109, 113
Tolbert, Charles M., 115
Treiman, Donald, 74
Tuchman, Barbara, 18
Tumin, Melvin, 63

Unemployment
  causes of, 54
  rates (tables), 55, 56, 57
Unit labor costs, 69
U.S.S.R. (*see* Command economies)

Vroom, Victor H., 77

Walder, Andrew, 110
Ware, Norman, 41

Watt, James (*see* Steam engine)
Weber, Max, 29
White, Lynn, 16, 17
Wittfogel, Karl, 6
Womack, James, 111
Women workers
  by age of children (table), 47
  labor force participation rates
    (table), 45
  by occupation (table), 50
Work outcomes, defined, 59 (*see also*
    Income; Prestige; Work
    satisfaction)
Work satisfaction
  distributions of (tables), 80, 81
  explanation of, 79–82
  and incentives, 78
  and productivity, 76–78
Writing, 7–8, 10
  bureaucratic applications of, 7, 10
  development of, 7–8, 10

WORK AND SOCIETY:
AN INTRODUCTION TO INDUSTRIAL SOCIOLOGY
Second Edition
Edited by Gloria Reardon
Production supervision by Kim Vander Steen
Cover design by Lesiak/Crampton Design, Park Ridge, Illinois
Composition by Point West, Inc., Carol Stream, Illinois
Paper, Publishers Vellum
Printed and bound by McNaughton & Gunn, Saline, Michigan